D1493518

A FIELD GUIDE IN COLOUR TO

GARDEN &
FIELD BIRDS

· EGGS & NESTS ·

A FIELD GUIDE IN COLOUR TO

GARDEN &
FIELD BIRDS

• EGGS & NESTS •

By Jiří Felix

Illustrated by Květoslav Hísek

CHANCELLOR
PRESS

Chapter on Migration by Dr John Sparks
Translated by Olga Kuthanová
Graphic design by Soňa Valoušková

Previously published in 1983 by
Octopus Books Limited
part of Reed International Books

This 1993 edition published by
Chancellor Press
Michelin House
81 Fulham Road
London SW3 6RB

Reprinted in 1994

ISBN 1 85152 128 3

Printed in Slovakia by Neografia, Martin

3/10/04/51-18

CONTENTS

FOREWORD

Birds are small, lively, sometimes brightly coloured creatures, occasionally having beautiful voices. They have long endeared themselves to man and it is no wonder that he wants to know their names, where they live and what they feed on. He has always been interested to distinguish between those which are useful and harmful — to learn what kind of nests they build and what their eggs look like. Some people even like to help birds, for instance, by providing food for them in winter or putting up nest boxes.

This book is the first of a four-volume series on European birds, divided according to habitats, i.e., the places where they occur. Each volume will cover 64 species of birds and the reader will thus be able to become acquainted with the 256 birds that regularly nest in Europe. The volumes will be divided as follows: 1) birds of gardens and fields. 2) birds of woods and mountains. 3) birds of meadows, swamps and inland water-courses. 4) birds of the sea and coastal regions.

The pictorial section of this book is further divided into three smaller sections: A) birds of built-up areas. B) birds of parks and gardens. C) birds of the field.

Naturally there will be a certain amount of overlap between the volumes. In the interests of dealing with the species only once, it has been necessary to describe each bird in the habitat where it is most usually found. The text accompanying the illustrations, nevertheless, will inform the reader of all the other places where the given species can be also found.

The grouping of the individual species of birds is thus determined by the habitats where they are usually found and where they nest. Exceptions have been made in the case of those birds that nest in the far north but regularly migrate, for instance, to central Europe in winter, where they occur in towns and cities, in trees bordering roads, in fields, etc. These so-called winter visitors are included in this volume even though they nest in different habitats. Two such examples are the waxwing and brambling. Parks and gardens also include overgrown cemeteries and avenues of trees, whereas fields also embrace field boundaries overgrown with thickets.

ABOUT BIRDS IN GENERAL

If we wish to learn something about birds and their ways of life we must first say a few words about their general characteristics. Birds are higher vertebrates with a constant and fairly high body temperature ranging from 38° to 44°C. depending upon the species. They have two pairs of limbs, the front pair being in the form of wings; these are usually used for flying. Some species of birds have frail wings incapable of supporting them in flight and adapted, say, for swimming — like the flippers of penguins. The great auk was a European example, at one time very common on the North Atlantic coasts, but now extinct. All other European birds are airborne species.

Birds evolved over millions of years from reptiles, with which they share many common features. For instance, both reptiles and birds lay eggs, have a comparable arrangement of the reproductive and excretory organs, the ducts of which share a common opening with the gut — the cloaca. The development of their embryos and certain aspects of their skeletons are also similar.

The first creatures to develop feathered wings appeared about 150 million years ago, in the Jurassic period of the Mesozoic. These primitive birds were called *Archaeopteryx* and were the size of a pigeon. *Archaeopteryx* possessed a bill provided with teeth and had a long tail composed of twenty-three vertebrae with feathers arranged on either side. Fossil remains of this bird were found in Upper Jurassic slate formations in Bavaria. *Archaeopteryx* was incapable of flying strongly, and probably used its wings chiefly for "parachuting" or gliding. It became extinct in the late Jurassic, and it is not known whether it was a direct link in the further evolution of birds.

The fossil of another extinct bird, *Hesperornis*, was also found in the North American Chalk of western Kansas. This species resembled the present day divers and was also incapable of flight, having finely toothed jaws, presumably to grasp fish. It lived between 100 and 125 million years ago. Other primitive birds living at this time included *Ichthyornis*, *Apatornis*, etc. Like the others these, too, did not survive the end of the Cretaceous period — when chalk was being deposited. The end of the Chalk Age marked the end of the Mesozoic era and onset of the Tertiary which brought with it many genera and species of birds, strange, often immense creatures that later became extinct, but also species greatly resembling those of the present day.

Sense Organs

Birds' sense organs exhibit various degrees of development. Some are highly developed whereas others are rudimentary. Of secondary importance, for instance, is the sense of taste, taste buds generally being located deeper inside the mouth on the soft upper palate and on the mucous membrane underneath the tongue. Birds do not chew their food, but tend to swallow it quickly, therefore hardly needing to taste it, as mammals do. The sense of smell is also very little developed. Most birds are not aware of scent. The kiwi is an exception.

The sense of touch is developed in varying degrees. Birds generally have such sensory organs inside the bill and underneath the tongue, but some have them also at the base of certain feathers, on the legs, etc. Birds that obtain their food from the ground, where they are unable to see clearly, even have these organs at the tip of the bill. Special sensory organs for registering heat and cold are located on the unfeathered parts of the body.

A bird's most perfect and important sensory organ is the eye. Birds see far better than other animals. The eye is large and focusses not only by means of muscles squeezing the lens as in the case of mammals, but also by flattening or bulging the transparent front of the eye — or cornea. The eyes are usually located on either side of the head and thus each has its own field of vision. Some birds, such as owls, however, have both eyes facing forward, so conferring a degree of stereoscopic vision. In addition to the upper and lower eyelid they have another special one which extends from the inner corner and can cover the entire eye (nictitating membrane). The retina has a greater density of sensory cells than the eye of man, more than five times as many in the case of predatory birds, thus enabling them to see their prey at great distances.

Another important sensory organ is the ear. In the interests of streamlining, the outer ear of birds has no lobe and is usually covered with feathers. A short external ear channel leads to the eardrum, on the inside of which is but one earbone, corresponding to the stirrup in the human ear. Despite this a bird's hearing is very good; in some species, notably the owls, it is excellent and put to good use in hunting prey at night.

The vocal organs, located at the lower end of the trachea, likewise play an important role in the life of birds. This organ, called the syrinx, is remarkably well developed in songbirds, but less so in other groups of birds which have a range of simple, rather unmusical, calls; some, such as the white stork, lack the muscles responsible for sound production and communicate by clapping their mandibles together.

Skeleton

The bird skeleton is not only remarkably strong but also light, some of the bones being hollow and filled with air. The long bones, in particular, are tubular and very strong, and their inner pneumatic filling, provided by air sacs, greatly reduces the weight of the whole skeleton — a very important factor in flight. The breastbone is remarkably well developed, and anchors the powerful muscles which raise and lower the wings.

The simplest form of flight is gliding, the lift generated by the outspread wings causing the bird to sink very slowly — moving forwards all the time. Provided the air is rising faster than the bird's sinking speed, then it can gain altitude. This happens when the bird soars in thermals. The other form of flight is flapping, which is effected by beating the wings and of course consumes a great deal of energy. The speed of flight varies according to the species and their wings are adapted accordingly. Birds with long, narrow, pointed wings, such as swifts, are faster fliers than those whose wings are short and broad (e.g. blackbirds).

Feathers

The body of a bird is covered with feathers. These, however, do not grow continually over the whole body surface but in definite tracts called pterylae, the intervening spaces being termed apteria. Since the latter are concealed by feathers they are not evident at first glance. The feathers that give the body its typical shape are called contour feathers, e.g. the primary and secondary flight feathers, covert and tail feathers. Such a feather (Fig. 1) has a long, firm yet flexible shaft bordered on both sides by a web composed of separate individual barbs, which in turn have rows of smaller barbules supplied with hooklets (Fig. 2). If the web is damaged in any way, as when the feather is caught by the claw of a predator, the bird strokes

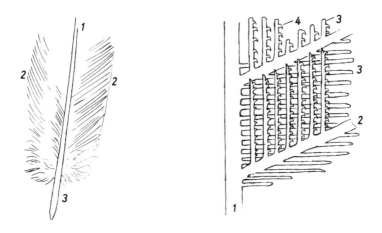

Fig. 1. Contour feather: 1) rachis, 2) vane, web, 3) quill.

Fig. 2. Arrangement of hooklets of a bird feather: 1) rachis, 2) barbules, 3) barbicels, 4) hooklets.

11

it with its bill or claws, thus causing the hooklets to catch and restore the web again. The tail feathers are likewise long and have strong hooks. Some birds, such as the woodpecker, have remarkably sturdy tail feathers which serve to support them on the tree trunk while they peck.

Underneath the contour feathers the body is usually covered with a layer of fine down feathers which are soft because the barbules do not possess hooklets. In many birds, e.g. ducks, these down feathers are very important during the nesting period for they are used to line the edges of the nest. During the temporary absence of the hen from the nest she covers the eggs with these feathers to prevent loss of heat.

Another type is the filament feather which is thin, almost hair-like, with a tip resembling a brush. This is generally found growing immediately next to the contour feathers. Finally, there are bristle feathers, found at the gape of certain birds. These have a short quill and are webless, probably serving to prevent the prey from escaping from the gape.

Feathers are variously coloured, this being basically of two kinds. One is caused by pigments, the other by the reflection of light from specially designed feathers and producing metallic hues (e.g. sheen on the "speculum" wing feathers of ducks). Sometimes there may be a total lack of pigment in which case the bird has white feathers. This is known as albinism, whereas an excess of black pigment resulting in dark coloration is called melanism. These aberrations may sometimes be incomplete — e.g. partial albinism may be seen in city blackbirds which are often striped white.

A bird's feathers are replaced regularly and this process is called moulting. The old feathers are shed as the new ones grow. Some birds moult once a year, the majority of songbirds and many other types twice yearly. As a rule, the contour feathers, e.g. the tail and flight feathers, are shed successively so that the bird does not lose its power of flight, thus becoming easy prey for raptors. However, some birds, such as ducks, go through a flightless period until new pinions and tail feathers grow, concealing themselves in reeds and rushes during the interval. Many birds have two differently coloured garbs a year.

One is the bright breeding plumage or nuptial dress, especially that of the males, the other the duller and drabber non-breeding winter or eclipse plumage. In some types of birds, e.g. ducks, the male loses his bright plumage following the breeding season and until the autumn months his coloration resembles that of the camouflaged female, at which time the contour feathers are again replaced, restoring him to his former glory.

Other birds have a different winter garb, donned in the autumn following a complete moult and replaced after a partial spring moult by the nuptial dress. Some examples of this are the bramblings, chaffinches, waders and gulls. The black-headed gull has a white-coloured head in winter which in adult birds turns chocolate-brown in early spring.

In some species the male and female exhibit a marked

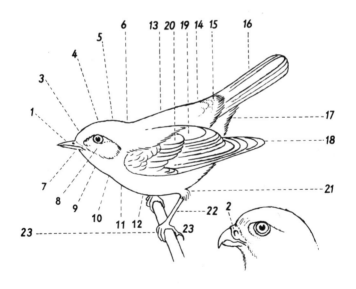

Fig. 3. Bird topography: 1) bill, 2) cere, 3) forehead, 4) crown, 5) nape, 6) hind neck, 7) lores, 8) cheeks, 9) throat, 10) crop, 11) breast, 12) belly, 13) back, 14) rump, 15) upper tail coverts, 16) tail feathers, 17) under tail coverts, 18) primaries, 19) secondaries, 20) wing coverts, 21) tibial feathers, 22) tarsus, 23) I.—IV. toe with claws.

difference in coloration (sexual dimorphism). Examples are the blackbird, mallard, house sparrow and pheasant. In other species the male and female have similar plumage and cannot be distinguished from each other at first glance, e.g. the song thrush, jackdaw, swift, and various kinds of tits.

Fig. 3 shows the different parts of a bird. Knowledge of the terms is useful in making detailed descriptions. The wing length is measured from the carpal or wrist joint to the tip of the longest primary. The body length is measured from the tip of the bill to the tip of the tail.

Bill

The bill, covered by a thick and strong horny sheath, is another important part of the bird's body. The individual bird groups exhibit marked variation in the shape of the bill depending on the kind of food they eat. Birds of prey have a down-curved upper mandible with sharp edges enabling them not only to tear their food but also to "cut" it. Ducks, on the other hand, have a broad flat bill with serrated edge serving to sieve food. Seed-eaters have a strong, hard, cone-shaped bill for husking seeds more easily, while insectivorous birds have a narrow, pointed bill with which they can penetrate various cracks and fissures in search of food. The long, pointed bill of herons and their allies is used as a harpoon when hunting. Some birds have an upward-curved bill, others a down-curved one, and specialists such as the crossbill have overlapping mandibles, to extract the seeds from fir cones. Some bills are adapted for catching fish, others for chiselling in between the shells of bivalve molluscs (e.g. oyster-catchers).

Nesting

Birds are not as carefree and independent as most people think. During the breeding season each pair of birds claims and defends a nesting ground or territory. These are established by fighting and displaying but once established, territorial boundaries are respected by neighbours.

Single birds of other species may usually trespass without notice because they are not direct rivals. Even if they seek food on the same territory they either collect food of a different kind or in other places. Song thrushes, for example, seek their food chiefly on the ground, blue tits on the branches of trees and tree creepers seek insects in the crevices of bark. All these birds, then, can live together without any conflict whatsoever.

Nesting territories vary in size, even amongst birds of the same species. The area may be determined by the abundance of food and the degree of competition for territories. In gardens territories tend to be smaller than those situated in woods. Small birds naturally have smaller nesting territories than larger species. Those of large raptors such as buzzards are very large indeed. The territory of small songbirds may extend outwards some 40—70 metres from the nest, although the nest need not be located in the exact centre of the territory. Its location depends where the suitable sites are. Birds nesting in tree cavities will have an easier task of dividing up the available territory by the provision of nest boxes at regular intervals.

Some birds, even songbirds, breed in colonies, siting their nests either close together or immediately above one another, e.g. the house martin. In such cases the birds' nesting territory is so small that it is limited just to the nest and its immediate vicinity. These birds, however, have no need for separate feeding territories; they are agile fliers, capable of sustained flight, and hunt their food in the air. They fly perhaps several kilometres from their nest in search of food above the surfaces of ponds, rivers, and so on. Colonial nesting, on the other hand, has certain advantages, such as joint defence against intruders.

The house martin, swift and other aerial hunters, however, are not the only colonial nesters. Some ground feeders, like rooks, often nest in large colonies, sometimes on the outskirts of small towns and villages. Although foraging in fields, they can nest in the relative safety of the tops of tall trees. Jackdaws, too, sometimes form large colonies in cities on church steeples or castle towers and they also must fly far afield in search of food.

Following the nesting season most birds abandon their territories and roam the countryside. Only a few species, like the robin, defend them even out of the breeding period.

How can birds tell if a certain territory is already occupied? One of the functions of song is to advertise territorial ownership. The male usually sings from some elevated post, often before he starts to build the nest, thus notifying other males of the same species that the place is taken. In the case of songbirds it is usually the male that seeks the nesting site, those of some species arriving from their winter quarters several days ahead of the females. The song, in unpaired birds, has another purpose — namely of attracting a mate. In some instances it may also serve the purpose of frightening off other males in the vicinity. A strong, healthy bird has a loud, rich song thus demonstrating his "superiority" over the weaker individuals of his kind. It is interesting to note that a weaker bird in the neighbourhood sometimes falls silent as soon as a strong male commences his song.

Besides song most birds also produce other sounds typical for the given species. Most important of these is the call note, used to communicate amongst themselves even out of the nesting season, when, as a rule, the males do not sing; females have the same call. In addition to this there are other sounds expressing fright or warning. All these various sounds are innate to the given species and produced even by young birds reared in captivity which have never heard the voices of their parents, but in the case of song the young of many species have to learn it from their elders. Some birds, like marsh warblers, tend to mimic phrases from other species, and incorporate these into their own songs.

Building the Nest and Laying Eggs

Although some species simply lay their eggs in a depression in the ground, most birds construct nests in which they will lay their eggs and rear their young. Some nests are quite elaborate, others are more simple. Special in their way are those built by birds nesting in cavities, such as woodpeckers, who excavate a hole in the trunk or strong branches of a tree and lay the eggs at the bottom of the cavity without even bothering to line it. Other birds seek out ready-made abandoned cavities or various cracks and holes, then move in and make their own nest there. Some birds need nothing more than a pile of stones, a hole in the ground, or a crack in a wall. A few very specialized species, such as cuckoos, lay their eggs in the nests of other birds, and leave the foster parents to incubate the eggs and rear the chicks.

In some species it is the female that builds the nest, in others both partners; sometimes the male builds the nest and the hen lines it.

Many birds build their nests on the branches of trees or bushes, often suspended in quite an ingenious manner. Some are shaped like a shallow bowl, others are spherical with a side entrance, sometimes in the form of a tunnel. Nests are generally built of plant material and lined with animal products such as feathers, hair, horsehair, and so on. Some birds use other material; for example the song thrush plasters the inside of its nest with mud, while others, such as the house martin and swallow, build the entire nest of mud, lining it with fine feathers, straw and the like.

The ability to construct a nest of a certain type is inborn or instinctive to the given species and birds need not be taught how to go about it. The nest built by a young bird for the first time in early spring is identical with that erected by an older, more experienced bird. Every finch builds a nest that not only has the same shape but is composed of similar materials and lined with mud mixed with saliva, just as every chiffchaff builds a box-like nest on the ground.

The nest is built fairly quickly, usually within a matter of days, and then the female can begin to lay the eggs. The hens of smaller species lay the eggs at intervals of one day until their clutches are completed, while those of larger species produce eggs at lengthier intervals, even up to three to five days. In many instances the size of the clutch is typical for a given species. Pigeons generally lay two eggs, shore-birds four, finches and their allies about five, thrushes likewise about five, whereas tits may have a clutch comprising anywhere from six to fourteen eggs or more. In species that lay a varying number of eggs the size of the clutch depends primarily on the abundance of food, and has obvious survival value for the brood.

Some birds have only one brood a year, whereas others, such as blackbirds and tits, have two. Some species are known to bear three broods and the house sparrow may even have four a year. As a rule, birds that live in the vicinity of human dwellings, where conditions are far more propitious from the point of view of food supply, have one brood more a year than, say, birds of the same species living in the woods.

All members of the same species usually produce similarly coloured and patterned eggs. The redstart, for instance, has greenish-blue eggs, those of the house martin are pure white, the song thrush has blue-green eggs sparsely spotted with black, and the eggs of the starling are always pale blue. Some species of birds may show a marked variation in the colouring of the eggs, but always within certain limits. Those of the house sparrow, for instance, generally have spots or blotches coloured pale grey to black-brown and all intervening shades. The eggs of the chaffinch are covered with red-brown spots but the ground colour may be tinged violet or a greenish hue.

As a rule the colouring of the eggs is adapted to the environment in which the bird nests. Birds nesting in cavities generally have white eggs. As they are concealed throughout the entire hatching period, they do not need the camouflage of those laid on the ground or in thickets. The eggs of such birds are usually marked so as to merge with their surroundings and escape the notice of enemies. There are, of course, exceptions. For example pigeons and doves have pure white eggs and build their nests in bushes and trees; but originally they probably nested in tree holes or rock fissures. Owls, too, have white eggs, even those that nest on the ground, like short-eared owls. The eggs of birds that nest in the open are provided with protective colouring. A typical example is the skylark, which nests on the ground in open fields. Although the nest is usually concealed by a tussock of grass, the eggs are well camouflaged, and difficult to spot.

Conspicuously coloured eggs would be easily spotted in open nests by sharp-eyed thieves, such as magpies or carrion crows.

The size of the eggs of each species varies within certain limits and is a determining factor that distinguishes, for example, the egg of the great tit from that of the blue tit. The average length of the former is 18 mm whereas that of the latter is only 16 mm; however, the smallest egg laid by a great tit has been measured at 16 mm whereas the largest egg of the blue tit has been measured at 17.8 mm. Such differences between the maximum and minimum dimensions, however, occur only rarely.

Incubation

Many birds start incubating after the last or penultimate egg has been laid and the young then hatch at about the same time. In some species, for example the birds of prey, the hen starts incubating as soon as she has laid the first egg and the young then hatch successively. In a clutch of five eggs laid every other day there will be a difference of a full ten days between the first and last hatched offspring. In larger clutches the last to hatch are usually unable to survive the competition of the older and stronger nestlings and die, unless the food supply is particularly good.

In many species of birds only the female incubates, being fed for the entire period by the male, whereas in some species the two take turns, changing places at regular intervals. In others the male helps only occasionally, and there are even known instances where the eggs are hatched by the male alone — for example the European dotterel and the phalaropes — but this is exceptional.

The length of the incubating period depends on the size of the bird. In the case of small birds it is from twelve to fifteen days, in larger birds increasing in proportion to size to about twenty days. Some incubate as long as eighty days. In each species, however, this period is of more or less constant duration. In small species variations of two to three days may be caused by external factors such as dampness, cold, heat. The rook, for example, incubates seventeen to twenty days, the thrush twelve to thirteen, but in exceptional cases also as long as sixteen days.

Nidicolous and Nidifugous Birds

The young peck their way out of the egg with the aid of the so-called "egg tooth", a projection on the upper mandible. This is used to cut away a small part of the egg shell. The "tooth" disappears shortly after hatching.

Birds are divided roughly into two separate groups according to how advanced the chicks are on hatching. The first group, known as nidicolous or altricial species, includes the songbirds, woodpeckers and pigeons, the second, known as nidifugous or precocial species, includes the ducks, geese and game birds.

The young of nidicolous species, especially songbirds, are unfeathered when they hatch, their practically naked bodies covered in parts only with a light down; also the eyes are not yet open. Such immature and helpless nestlings are entirely dependent on the parents for food at least until they leave the nest. More usually the parents continue feeding them for some time afterwards until they are fully independent. The young of some birds, e.g. the thrushes and their allies, leave the nest while yet unable to fly, remaining and hiding on the ground where the parent birds bring them food. One will thus frequently come across a thrush or blackbird nestling on the ground; contrary to the popular belief, it has not fallen out of the nest.

The young of nidifugous birds already show a marked degree of development on hatching and can often run and usually feed themselves from the very first day. However, they are watched over and guided by the parent birds to spots where food is to be found and sheltered and kept warm under their wings at night and in bad weather. Thus, even the young of nidifugous species, like quail and partridges, are dependent on the care of their parents for a certain time.

When they are full-grown the young generally abandon their

home whereas the parents remain, often producing another brood. In the spring of the ensuing year the elder birds may return again to the same places whereas young nesters tend to seek new territories of their own. In swans and geese, the young remain in the company of their parents until the mating season the following spring. They are birds that form flocks in late summer or autumn and roam the countryside.

The prospect for survival of a young bird is not good. The majority die in their first year. For example, on average only 13 per cent of the great tit's offspring survive till the following spring and in the case of the redstart 30 per cent. Enough live to replace the mortality amongst the older birds, thus maintaining the bird population around a certain level. An adverse effect is likewise caused by man when he destroys the birds' nesting sites. Protection of birds is therefore essential if we are to preserve these creatures, in many instances very useful to man.

MIGRATION

Early Theories

The appearance and disappearance of certain kinds of birds with the changing of the seasons has always been a subject of comment and speculation; early observers were, however, at a loss to explain the phenomenon. An old sixteenth-century illustration shows fishermen working a net containing both fish and birds, which was presumably in accordance with the then popular belief that swallows overwintered in the bottoms of ponds. Others thought that cuckoos turned into hawks. Another theory was that in autumn birds flew to the moon, an idea as preposterous as it was quaint, and one which should have been finally exploded by the observations of the Apollo astronauts!

What is Migration?

Although there is one species which does hibernate the winter away — the North American poor-will (a nightjar or night hawk) — it is now well known that the seasonal coming and going of some species is due to the fact that their populations have two home ranges; a breeding range, and one which they occupy outside the breeding season. These ranges may overlap to some extent, but this does not alter the situation; *migration* is the bi-annual movement of populations of birds between their breeding and non-breeding ranges. Other mass movements of birds, such as those due to hard weather, irruptions and no-madic dispersal, will not be referred to here.

Migratory species that breed in the Northern hemisphere tend to move southwards to spend their off seasons in warm areas, some near, or even south of the equator. In the Southern hemisphere the reverse is true; the long-tailed cuckoo nests in New Zealand between October and March (the southern spring and summer), and then flies northwards to Melanesia where it spends the rest of the year. An exception to these patterns is the dainty Ross's gull, which spends the winter in the Arctic seas and migrates *south* to breed on the well wooded marshes of Siberian rivers, a movement that is more characteristic of Southern hemisphere species.

Not all birds take strongly lateral migratory flights. Arctic warblers, small leaf warblers inhabiting birch and coniferous forest as far west as Arctic Norway, travel to south-eastern Asia after the breeding season. The Siberian race of the willow warbler flies 13,000 km across Asia to winter in East Africa, a remarkable journey for a bird weighing less than 40 grams.

Long Distance Travellers

Many species make transequatorial journeys of staggering proportions. The most impressive of the world's long distance travellers is surely the arctic tern, a species that has an extensive breeding range in northern Europe and North America. Those that breed as far north as latitude 82°N travel down the Atlantic coast of Europe and Africa to the Antarctic seas at 74°S. The round trip is at least 35,000 km as the "crow" flies — but of course terns do not fly in straight lines! Giant petrels and many albatrosses spend their lives circumnavigating the globe in the teeth of the "roaring forties" and other trade winds. The migration routes of the migratory European birds of prey and many white storks tend to converge on the Near East because they are efficient soarers, not long distance flappers, and so tend to avoid crossing the Mediterranean Sea where there are no thermals to assist them. In autumn, 6,650 honey buzzards have been counted crossing the Bosphorus, near Istanbul, in a single day.

Some land based birds are also great travellers. The Pacific golden plover nests in the Alaskan tundra, and winters in Hawaii and Tonga, 3,000 km away in the central Pacific, thus requiring not only stamina but also very accurate navigation.

Needle-tailed swifts bi-annually make the 10,000 or 11,000 km journey between their breeding grounds in Siberia and Australia where they spend their off-season.

Why Migrate?

The value of migration to certain birds is not too difficult to understand. By migrating, some birds are able to take advantage of food supplies that are only seasonally abundant in certain areas. It seems that the more temperate and tropical areas can provide a stable and reliable food supply throughout the year, so species that nest there do not need to emigrate in their off--season. Migration is thus a phenomenon that tends to be associated with birds that nest in the higher latitudes.

This is particularly true for insectivorous birds. In late autumn and winter, insects are in short supply over much of northern Europe, Asia and North America, but in spring there is a glut. Therefore by moving in at this time of the year, a host of chats, warblers, martins, flycatchers, etc. can exploit this rich source of food to rear their ravenous youngsters. Similarly, the plankton and land flora bloom, encouraging an increased fish and mammal population respectively. At the same time wild-fowl, seabirds, raptors and many other small perching birds move northwards to breed, and after they have nested, when the days draw shorter, have to travel south again or else starve. Migration thus takes place for reasons of survival in these high latitudes. The survival value of long distance, transequatorial migrations therefore becomes evident; they enable some species to live in a perpetual summer of plenty!

European swallows, having raised perhaps two broods in the northern summer, spend the remainder of their year recuperating 8,000 km away in the South African summer, where insects are still plentiful. Although they may seem incredible to us, the fantastic journeys of the muttonbird and arctic tern are, despite the energy they use, in the birds' own interest. The theory of evolution and our acceptance of the process of natural selection leave us with no option but to suppose that the arctic tern's best chance of living and of producing chicks next year is to fly down to the edge of Antarctica and fatten up on the abundant krill in those southern seas.

Vertical migrations of species inhabiting mountainous regions can also be interpreted along the same lines; the white-capped redstart nests up to 4,000 metres in the Himalayas, but afterwards escapes the icy grip of winter by moving several hundred metres lower into the more hospitable foothills. Similarly, in Europe, the insectivorous wallcreeper with its gorgeous red epaulets may descend into the valleys where the hunting is easier during the winter.

For many birds, migration does not necessarily involve tremendously long flights. For instance, redwings and fieldfares — thrushes which breed in the extreme north of Europe — merely move a few hundred or perhaps a thousand kilometres to escape the worst of the winter in the north of their range. These thrushes invade the British Isles to spend the winter there and take advantage of the mild oceanic climate. Some widely distributed species are also only migratory in parts of their range. Robins and blackbirds are regular migrants in Europe, but the British sub-species of both are more or less sedentary. The less harsh weather conditions have not favoured the evolution of migratory behaviour in the British breeders.

What Causes the Migration Urge?

The factor which triggers off migration is almost certainly the changing hours of daylight. Birds, and many other animals, are extremely sensitive to the changing "photo period", as it is called. In autumn, the rapidly shortening days bring about an alteration in the birds' hormonal balance which causes them to lay down reserves of fat. Also they become restless, and their character changes. Territorial species may become highly sociable, and the massing of swallows in flocks are familiar signs of pre-migratory behaviour.

When weather conditions are suitable, migration begins, and the birds then respond to a set of instructions in their nervous systems, inherited from and perfected by the trial and error of countless generations. Natural selection becomes very rigorous during migration periods. One can imagine that any weaklings among the small land birds in western Europe which set off on long migratory flights in hostile weather conditions, or in a direction taking them on a hopeless course into the Atlantic, would very quickly be weeded out. Thus we know that in autumn, warblers, chats and flycatchers start their journey south from Scandinavia when anticyclonic conditions prevail over the North Sea, bringing clear skies and light, and favourable, or at least no unfavourable winds. Other weather systems may conceal squawls and gale force head winds over the North Sea, which take a tremendous toll of migrants.

Birds may not be conscious weather prophets, but migration is doubtless triggered off in birds in the migrating mood by a certain favourable combination of external events. These will, of course, vary from species to species and from place to place.

Tracking Migrants

No-one can fail to be inspired by the sight of birds on migration, and it is, therefore, not surprising that ornithologists have devoted a great deal of energy to recording their movements. Many bird observatories are placed at strategic points in the avian flyways. Cap Gris Nez on the northern coast of France is a natural departure point for passerines leaving the continent of Europe to overwinter in the British Isles. In autumn, vast flocks of starlings and chaffinches can be seen winging their way up into the sky, perhaps in the face of strong westerly winds, to make the Channel crossing; while beneath them thousands of dumpy common scoter, mainly from the Baltic, pass in long lines hugging the wave tops on their journey westwards. Visible migration over the island of Falstarbo in the Baltic reaches staggering proportions, as chaffinches, bramblings, starlings and raptors flee south before the implacable march of winter.

From direct observations it is possible to map out the major migration routes of certain species

A further sophistication of direct observation has come in with the use of high-powered radar equipment, which is of tremendous value in monitoring migration. Flocks of birds show up as spots on the screen, or Plan Position Indicator, and for the first time it has been possible to see quite clearly the extent of avian traffic by night. Many species tend to feed during the day and travel only when it is dark, and warblers, thrushes and waders all tend to start their journeys during the evening. It is also quite apparent that the vast majority of birds migrate at heights which render them invisible from the ground. Over England, the most frequent altitude seems to be around 900—1,000 metres, although a considerable amount of avian traffic occurs well above this height. Incidentally, a number of species like the Siberian white crane must regularly cross the Himalayas and reach heights of around 4,700 metres on bi-annual journeys to and from their breeding grounds.

Radar watches have shown how certain land birds, like wheatears and thrushes, tend to lose altitude at night while crossing open sea, and then gain height at dawn. They have even cast some doubt upon the validity of information obtained by ground observation about visible migration. Very often it seems as though the main high altitude bird movements as tracked by radar bear little relation to what ornithologists report from sea level where low flying birds may represent the "lost" ones that have become disorientated.

Ringing, or bird banding, is perhaps the technique that has been most helpful to us in finding out where birds go when they are migrating. The first large-scale ringing scheme was started in 1899 in Denmark and since then millions of birds have been individually tagged. In the British Isles alone, between 1909 and 1968, nearly 6,400,000 birds were ringed and 171,520 recovered. By plotting the recoveries, it is possible to build up a picture of the pattern of dispersal of each species. Occasionally ringing recoveries will provide us with information that it would be impossible to obtain by any other method. For example, the three breeding populations of barnacle geese do not intermingle during the winter, but have their separate winter feeding ranges.

How fast?

The other advantage of being able to recognize individuals is that the recoveries provide information on the *speed* at which migrants make their journeys. A blue-winged teal ringed in North America has been known to cover at least 6,000 km in one month, which is an average of 200 km a day. Even this record is dwarfed into insignificance by the recent report of a knot (a wading bird) ringed in the British Isles and recovered eight days later, 5,800 km away, in Liberia.

It seems likely that many species are "long haul" migrants that are capable of sustaining flight for at least one or two days before refuelling. It is clear that some perching birds must make considerable flights over the sea before reaching land; for example Greenland wheatears, which are larger and rather longer in the wing than the ones nesting on the mainland of Europe, probably fly directly across 3,000 km of the North Atlantic in the autumn to make a landfall in Spain.

We have already shown that migrating birds can make long distance flights, and some do so from necessity. For instance, the Pacific race of the American golden plover flies directly from its Canadian breeding grounds to winter in Hawaii, a journey of 3,000 km, and one that would do credit to many airliners! Like aircraft, birds need fuel; long haul species like sanderling, curlew, sandpiper and knot accumulate fat before migrating, and it may account for 50 per cent of their body weight when they leave. From what is known about the energy requirements of birds, it has been calculated that one weighing 20 gms with a maximum load of fat could have a theoretical flight range of between 2,100 and 5,900 km! Migrants that habitually make their journeys in small stages accumulate lighter loads of body fat; these can "refuel" *en route*.

Living Compasses

Perhaps the most puzzling feature of migration is how birds find their way across the surface of the earth so successfully. Some of the feats of navigation are really quite remarkable; bristle-thighed curlews, which nest in the high Canadian tundra, find their way to Tahiti, a mere pin-point in the middle of the Pacific, to winter there (see also the case of the Pacific golden plover).

Most people are aware of the feats of homing shown by racing pigeons, but their abilities are nothing compared with the amazing accomplishments of wild birds artificially released from their nest sites. A Manx shearwater removed from its burrow on the Welsh island of Stockholm, and released at Boston Airport, made the 5,080 km flight across the trackless Atlantic to its nest in $12\frac{1}{2}$ days. 18 Laysan albatrosses removed from their nesting quarters on Midway Island in the central Pacific were released at distances up to 6,600 km away. 14 returned at speeds of up to 507 km a day!

It is, therefore, quite apparent that birds must have a very accurate means of assessing where they are on the surface of the earth in relation to their home base or destination. Various theories have been put forward over the years — such as, that birds are able to navigate by means of Corioli's Force or by being directly influenced by the earth's magnetic field.

However, a great mass of scientific data has now been accumulated which supports the view that birds use both the sun and the stars as navigation beacons, and this explains why migrants become so disorientated if they run into overcast or foggy conditions. Over twenty years ago it was discovered by Gustav Kramer that during the period of normal migration captive starlings would establish themselves in their cage in the direction they should be travelling in — providing they could see the sun. By a suitable arrangement of mirrors, the apparent position of the sun could be altered, and this was reflected in corresponding changes in the starling's position.

Of course, much migration takes place at night and again, it seems that celestial clues are used. Captive blackcaps and garden warblers flutter predominantly in south-westerly and north-easterly directions in the autumn and spring respectively, providing they can see a part of the clear night sky. The pattern of "fixed" stars provides the clues, a fact substantiated by placing birds in planetaria. When the appropriate night sky was projected, the birds orientated themselves in the right migrating direction. Then, as the star pattern changed to another sky appropriate to a point where the species are known to be likely to change direction, the birds accordingly altered their course.

In order to use celestial clues, birds must have an accurate sense of timing to make allowances for the change in direction of the sun or stars as the day or night progresses. It would seem that they possess an internal biological clock. With their extremely sensitive vision, it is likely that by watching the sun for a very short period, a species like the Manx shearwater can compute the highest point on the arc (i.e. its position at mid-day). When the bird is removed from its home base, the comparison between the highest elevation of the sun at the point of release and at the home base will give information about the bird's relative latitude. If the sun is too high then it must fly north; if it is too low then it must strike out to the south. Information about its longitudinal position will be revealed by its biological clock. If the sun appears to be too far on its daily course across the sky at any given moment, the bird must be too far west in relation to its home base, and so on.

Migration is an infinitely more subtle business than flying on a fixed heading. Many migration routes are far from straight and the air is rarely still, and birds must be able to compensate for drift. Experience also counts for something; the adults which have already made the journey may possibly remember certain landmarks, and may even be able to reorientate more successfully when they have drifted off course; on the other hand the juveniles of migrating species can take up the appropriate course without apparent trouble. Several thousand starlings were trapped in Holland while migrating south-west, and they were ringed and released several hundred kilometres away in Switzerland. The results were very interesting; the immature birds continued headlong on their south-western course and were recovered in south-western France and Spain, while the adults apparently reorientated north-west and thus compensated for their displacement. Next spring, the immatures apparently returned to the area of their birth, but in subsequent years, they continued to overwinter in south-western France and Spain!

Some young birds, like cuckoos, can get no guidance from the adults because they have gone on ahead of their offspring. This is precisely what makes migration so fascinating. Many migratory birds have a brain that can sit comfortably on a thumb nail, and yet when only a few months old can expedite journeys of fantastic proportions and can, with such apparent expertise, reach places of which they cannot have had any prior knowledge or experience.

BIRDS IN BUILT-UP AREAS

Countless species of birds congregate in built-up areas. Many have found suitable nesting sites on buildings, others have been attracted by the availability of food. Some species have even taken advantage of the favourable conditions man unknowingly has prepared for them and have multiplied at a fantastic rate sometimes nearing catastrophic proportions. A typical example is the house sparrow, which has associated itself with man, probably from the time grain was first cultivated and thus became the first species to settle permanently with us.

The house sparrow is not universally popular because throughout the year 80 per cent of its diet consists of grain kernels; furthermore it snips off the buds of fruit trees and shrubs and also feeds on young lettuce plants. Even though it feeds its young on insects and their larvae or caterpillars during the nesting season this nowhere near balances its harmful activities. In large cities it is an especially unwelcome visitor to markets, where it may soil food and also foul stalls and equipment. Experts have still not been able to solve the long-standing problem of the sparrow. There are records from the 18th century revealing that the killing of sparrows was mandatory in many European countries at that time and that farmers had to deliver a specified number of sparrow heads to the authorities as proof of their obeying this order. The house sparrow is furthermore very quarrelsome, chasing away other birds and often usurping nest boxes set up for species such as tits.

Nowadays the house sparrow is found even in the heart of large cities, on bustling main streets and squares, where other birds would be quite incapable of existing. It adapted itself to this new environment with amazing rapidity and began to feed on all kinds of food remnants of both animal and plant origin. With its excellent opportunistic powers it has even learned to "deal" with man, seeming to gauge instinctively how close it can safely approach. In a park, for example, it will cheekily perch on benches or hop up to accept food from the hand. Elsewhere it keeps its distance, retaining a certain wariness.

The blackbird too is regularly found in the company of man but its "domestication" occurred much later than that of the house sparrow. In 1855 ornithologists were still describing the blackbird as a very shy woodland bird. After that it gradually began to set up home in parks and gardens with increasing frequency, but only quite recently did it begin to invade the outskirts of towns and penetrate parks in city centres. Finally it began to make its home even in small backyards with a few thick shrubs and trees. Living close to man also markedly affected the blackbird's migratory habits. In northern Europe, but not the British Isles, the blackbird migrated south-west and spent the winter months in the countries bordering the Mediterranean. Only a certain number of males remained in their nesting grounds during the winter months. Now, however, not only older males but also a number of younger individuals as well as females remain throughout the year. Blackbirds faithful to their original habitat in the woods still migrate to warmer regions in great numbers.

Nowadays blackbirds in urban areas build their nests not only in thickets and trees but also directly on roofs, windowsills, balconies, rafters in sheds, open letter boxes and other convenient sites. The comings and goings of passers-by do not deter them and a sitting hen is sometimes so unafraid that she will allow herself to be stroked. In winter blackbirds often visit window feeders and gardens and have even become tame enough to take food scraps from our dinner tables. This unnatural fare is obviously to their liking and causes no problems of digestion. Blackbirds have even been observed visiting window feeders in early spring, filching titbits for their young.

Many blackbirds' nests in cities are destroyed by cats, which often kill hundreds of young nestlings in the parks. The birds, however, ensure the preservation of the species by building a new nest and raising another brood. It is interesting to note that blackbirds in cities multiply particularly rapidly. They have more nestlings and more broods in a year than do those that make their home in woodlands for they have ample food and a warmer environment. Blackbird populations in cities are continually increasing in number, and one may often see pure white or more often partially albino individuals.

During the past few decades the song thrush is also becoming a city bird, even though the majority are still woodland inhabitants. Every year, however, this bird becomes a more frequent visitor to parks and gardens and builds its nest in the immediate vicinity of houses. Unlike the blackbird it is still a migrant, but returns to its nesting grounds very early in the spring.

The swallow, a native of rocky localities which used to build its nest under rock overhangs or at the edges of caves, has almost entirely abandoned its original habitat. In Europe it is very seldom found in such places, having become increasingly accustomed to man's presence. Swallows have in fact even invaded his homes and out-buildings, constructing nests in cowsheds, barns, corridors — even bathrooms and living rooms! It is not disturbed too much by the presence of human beings, requiring only a partially open window through which it can fly in and out. It is of course far safer indoors, especially at night, when it is virtually immune from attacks by an owl. But modern housing developments afford few nesting opportunities and as a result this graceful, beautiful bird is less frequently seen in built-up areas. It is much more abundant in the country, where it finds not only suitable nesting sites but also an ample supply of nutritious insects.

The house martin has also invaded man's domain. Whole colonies often build their nests on the walls of houses, under the eaves, below balconies and so forth. In big cities, however, though until quite recently it still nested in large numbers, even above busy streets, it is now a less frequent visitor. The main reason for this appears to be the absence of abundant insect supplies in the fume-laden city skies. With the introduction of the Clean Air Act, however, house martins have started to nest once again in London after a long absence.

Another bird that has sought built-up areas from time to time is the Alpine swift. Originally an inhabitant of rocky regions, this bird's visits to some southern European cities have been limited only to fairly inaccessible places such as the eaves of tall buildings, granaries, towers, cracks in high walls, and the like. It seeks no closer ties with man.

A more familiar spring visitor to parks, gardens and back-yards (preferably furnished with nest boxes) is the starling. Should it not find such a box, it will often content itself with a hole in the wall. Originally a woodland bird, nesting in the cavities of tree trunks or holes in tree branches, the starling too has adapted to its new environment, without necessarily abandoning its rural habitat.

Two other birds, the black redstart and common redstart, which both fly south for the winter, are seen with increasing frequency in built-up areas. On the continent of Europe the former, in particular, may often be found in the backyards of village houses and it also nests on the outskirts of large cities, where it is content to occupy a hole in the wall left by a dis-lodged brick or better still a nest box hung up for its use. Originally black redstarts inhabited only high mountain slopes, where they may sometimes be seen even today, but the majority nowadays seem to prefer village and town surroundings and are settling in the lowlands. The common redstart shows this tendency to a somewhat lesser degree, and is to be found chiefly in parks and established gardens.

High on most people's list of popular park and garden birds, though just as often found in woods, is the chaffinch, which is sometimes sufficiently tame to take food from the hand, espe-cially in winter, for in summer, as a rule, it has ample nourish-ment. The song of the male in the breeding season is particularly delightful. The reason for its frequenting built-up areas is probably to be found in a sudden increase in population, necessitating a search for new places to raise a brood. This explanation is borne out by the fact that in recent years the chaffinch has put in an appearance in northern areas where it was previously non-existent. Nowadays its distribution extends as far as the Arctic Circle.

The serin too has not only shifted its range to the neighbour-hood of towns and villages but has likewise expanded its distribution to cover the whole of Europe. This small bird is a common inhabitant of parks and gardens and in fact will not venture far from houses and other buildings, often nesting in trees adjoining busy streets and highways. In the 17th century the serin's European range was restricted to the Mediterranean countries but around 1800 the population began spreading rapidly northward across the Alps and even further. It returned as a migrant to its original home in the south every winter but with the arrival of spring again moved to new places, its range expanding year by year. In 1922 it began to nest in Holland. In 1942 it made its first appearance in southern Sweden and in 1949 it showed up in Denmark. Since then it has even begun to settle in mountain areas, nesting at altitudes as high as 1350 metres above sea level. But it was not until 1967 that a pair of serins were recorded breeding in southern England.

Even more striking is the spread of another alien in Europe, the collared dove, associated with man throughout the whole year. A native of India and western and southern China, it was introduced to Asia Minor in the 16th century where it was kept in semi-captivity at the courts of the various sultans, who treated it as a protected species. Thus privileged, it began to move freely about in cities. It is recorded that the Turkish emperor gave a pair of doves to Henry II of France on the occasion of his coronation in 1547. Later, in the 18th century, the collared dove began to spread farther across Asia Minor and at the same time eastwards as far as Japan. Westward its range soon included Bulgaria and then the whole of the Balkan peninsula. Subsequently it appeared in larger cities such as Bucharest, Budapest, Bratislava, Prague, Hanover, Munich and in 1951 even as far north as Rostock. Birds ringed in Bohemia were retrieved months later in Belgium and West Germany.

In 1952 the collared dove appeared for the first time in England; in 1954 it had made its way as far as Norway and Scotland and in 1964 it reached what is thus far its most northern point of distribution — Iceland. In these areas too it lives alongside man in town and village, rapidly becoming established, multiplying at an amazing rate and seemingly impervious to long, hard winters. To this day no one is able to explain what prompted the dove to leave its home in the warm climate of India and later to spread north-west at such an astonishing speed from south-east Europe. Within the space of a few years it has colonised the whole of Europe, settling chiefly in built-up areas. Will its expansion continue and will it even find its way to America? The answer to that question will be revealed during the next few years.

Certain corvine birds are likewise common inhabitants of today's European cities. First and foremost is the jackdaw, which nests on church steeples and castle turrets. Most jackdaws still settle in localities where there are plenty of old trees and tree cavities or rocks. Sometimes they establish themselves in old parks near rookeries. The rook is also sometimes a city inhabitant. All it needs is a small park or garden with a few old tall trees. Of course it cannot find sufficient food there and has to fly to the fields and meadows far beyond the city outskirts. What led it to take up residence in cities, however, remains a mystery.

Other small birds that have moved in with man are the tits, mainly the great tit and the blue tit. Both nest not only in nest boxes put up in parks and gardens but also in cracks in the walls of buildings, hollow fence poles and even in letter boxes. In winter the great and blue tits are daily visitors to window feeding trays and bird tables.

In the country and on the outskirts of large cities one will often find also the pied and grey wagtails nesting near houses as well as many other songbirds which build their nests in parks and gardens.

Certain woodpeckers are likewise found in parks and gardens, e.g. the great spotted, grey-headed and green woodpeckers. In southern Europe the wryneck often makes a home in a garden nest box, for, unlike the woodpecker, it does not chip out its own cavity, and its melodious call note in spring is a familiar sound.

It is not uncommon to find birds of prey, such as kestrels, in cities, though open country is preferred. This small predator often raises its brood on the high towers of churches or castles, frequently in the very heart of large cities. One or two pairs regularly nest in central London.

Some owls have likewise taken to nesting in the vicinity of human dwellings. The tawny owl has adapted to city life best of all. Barn owls may nest in attics and occupied dovecots, and even in church or clock towers, apparently undisturbed by the regular pealing of bells or chiming of the hour.

Each year, an increasing number of birds set up home alongside man — wherever they can find suitable living conditions and nesting opportunities. In western Europe, in recent years, such species have included the carrion crow, mistle thrush, wood pigeon and moorhen. Birds not only brighten our lives with their presence and melodious songs, but are also beneficial in that they destroy quantities of garden pests.

PLATES

The plates depict 64 species of birds. In those cases where the coloration of the male differs from that of the female (sexual dimorphism) both are shown. Also included is a colour illustration of the typical egg of the given species and sometimes a pen-and-ink drawing of the nest. The plates are arranged according to the birds' biotopes and within each group according to the zoological system of classification. The text accompanying each plate gives the basic biological data about the given species as well as items of particular interest. The column at top right gives the average length of the bird in centimetres, measured from the tip of the bill to the tip of the tail, the bird's coloration, a verbal transcription of the song and dimensions of the egg. These dimensions are given in millimetres, e.g. $14.8-18.2 \times 10.3-12.2$ mm, the first figure denoting the minimum length of the egg, the second the maximum length, the third the minimum width and the fourth the maximum width.

Song Thrush

Turdidae

Turdus philomelos

One cold morning in March one may hear a loud flute-like song. It is the male song thrush, returned from its winter quarters in North Africa and southern Europe and proclaiming its ownership of nesting territory. The birds perch on the branches of trees, as yet still bare, making them all the more conspicuous. Not until several days later are they joined by the females who select their mates with nesting ground already staked out. The song thrush may frequently be seen not only in parks and gardens but also in woods. In the middle of April its nest of dry plant stems may be found in trees, among thickets as well as on shed rafters. It is easily recognized by the interior of mud and rotting wood cemented together with saliva and forming a smooth layer that soon dries and turns hard. It is provided with no further lining. The four to six eggs are incubated by the hen for twelve to fourteen days, the hatched nestlings being fed in the nest by both parents for two weeks. After this time they hop out of the nest, remaining on the ground and continuing to be provided with food by the adults. This consists of worms, snails, caterpillars and also berries. In late September or early October the thrushes, inhabiting almost the whole of Europe, leave for their winter quarters.

Length: 23 cm.
Voice: A loud "tchuck" or "tchick", sometimes "dag--dag".
Song: Flute-like, whistling, very distinctive varied phrases, repeated two to four times, between brief pauses.
Size of Egg: 23.0—31.8× ×18.6—23.0 mm.

European Blackbird

Turdus merula

The blackbird is found in all but the northernmost parts of Europe. In central and western Europe it is mostly resident, but more northern populations winter in the Mediterranean. In spring, at dawn and even while it is still dark, one may hear the melodic song of the male perched on a rooftop, a tall post or a tree. The song may be interspersed with various other sounds, for the bird is an expert mimic. As soon as the thickets show the first hint of green he begins building his nest of roots, grass stems, bits of paper and rags, often using mud as well. The nest may be found in many different places — in thickets or trees, on a windowsill or wall, in a pile of wood, etc. In the latter part of April the hen may already start incubating the four to six eggs. The young hatch after thirteen to fifteen days, leaving the nest two weeks later, as yet incapable of flight, and concealing themselves on the ground. The parent birds are tireless providers of food, mainly earthworms, which they are very adept at pulling out of the ground. Blackbirds also feed on caterpillars, molluscs and, in autumn and winter, berries as well as scraps from the dinner table. In winter they are frequent visitors to window feeders as well as feeding trays in parks and gardens.

Length: 25.5 cm. Sexual dimorphism. *Voice:* "tchink, tchink, tchink"; an anxious "tchook". *Song:* Loud, flute-like, very melodic; the male sings from a high perch. *Size of Egg:* 24.0—35.5× ×18.0—23.6 mm. Male in foreground, female behind.

42

Common Redstart

Phoenicurus phoenicurus

Turdidae

In the first half of April the common redstart returns to its nesting grounds throughout the whole of Europe, having travelled all the way from tropical Africa where it has spent the winter months (the outward journey having been started in September or early October). It frequents sun--dappled woods but is mainly to be seen in parks and occasionally town gardens. It makes its presence known soon after arrival, for it is a very agile bird, hardly still for a moment and contin-ually twitching its tail. The male, singing his rasping song, is seen on the roofs of houses, sheds and similar buildings. The nest is built in May in wall crevices, among the rafters beneath a shed roof, or in the free spaces between stacked wood. Failing such sites, the redstart will also take advantage of a nest box. The nest is made of roots, plant stalks, moss and leaves and lined with hairs and feathers. The hen lays five to eight eggs which she incubates alone for thirteen to fifteen days. On hatching, the ever hungry nest-lings pose quite a problem for their parents who are seemingly tireless in bringing them young caterpillars, butterflies, bed bugs, beetles and other insects, many caught on the wing. The young leave the nest after twelve to sixteen days and soon afterwards the parents begin to prepare for a second brood.

Length: 14 cm.
Sexual dimorphism.
Voice: A sharp "tooick", a liquid "wheet" and "whee-tic-tic".
Song: Lengthy high note followed by two lower--pitched short sounds — otherwise varying according to the individual.
Size of Egg: 16.1—21.0× ×12.3—15.1 mm.
Male above, female below.

44

Black Redstart

Phoenicurus ochruros

In late March black redstarts return to their nest sites in built-up areas. It was originally a native of cliffs and mountain regions, where it still occurs. The black redstart is, however, a very rare breeding species in south-eastern England. It builds its nest in wall crevices, behind drainpipes and on windowsills but will welcome even a semi--nest box and on rare occasions will even nest in a tree cavity. It remains faithful to its nesting ground, returning there every year throughout its lifetime. The nest, built in practically the same spot each time, consists of bits of twigs, roots, plant stalks, dry leaves and mud, and is lined with fine hairs. The hen usually lays five eggs, incubating them herself for thirteen to fourteen days, while the male rasps his song from a high perch nearby. The neighbourhood surrounding stables, sties and rubbish dumps is the black redstart's favourite hunting ground, offering an abundance of insects to be caught on the wing and fed to the young. The chicks often leave the nest as early as twelve days after hatching, though yet unable to fly, and conceal themselves on the ground. In October the black redstart leaves for its winter quarters in the Mediterranean. Only individuals inhabiting western and southern Europe are resident.

Length: 14 cm. Sexual dimorphism. *Voice:* A stuttering "tititic" and a brief "tsip"; warning: "fuid, teck-teck". *Song:* Rasping and chirping, sometimes with flute-like notes. *Size of Egg:* 17.0—21.5× ×13.2—16.2 mm. Colour generally white, sometimes with inconspicuous rusty spots. Male above, female on nest.

Great Tit

Parus major

Paridae

The great tit may be found in all parks and gardens, even in the immediate vicinity of buildings, as well as in woodlands. Its distribution includes the whole of Europe and a large part of Asia and North Africa. Most do not leave their nesting grounds even in winter and only tits inhabiting the northernmost areas sometimes fly south-west in small flocks in the autumn. As early as April and then again in June or July it builds its soft-
-lined nest in tree cavities, wall crevices as well as nest boxes. First it gathers bits of moss and lichen and then lines a deep hollow with fine hairs and feathers. When all is ready the hen lays one egg a day until there are eight to ten, at which stage she begins incubating. The male does not assist her in this task but brings her a juicy caterpillar at intervals to satisfy her hunger. The naked, helpless nestlings hatch after thirteen to fourteen days and the parent birds are kept busy supplying them with food, mainly caterpillars. During the first few days they make as many as five hundred trips a day and before the nestlings are fledged even eight hundred a day. The young tits abandon the nest at the age of sixteen to twenty-one days but perch on branches close by for several more days, continuing to be fed by the parent birds. In winter the great tit is one of the commonest visitors to bird tables.

Length: 14 cm.
Voice: A clear "tsink, tsink", "tchair, tchair" or "chi-chi-chi".
Song: Ringing "teechew, teechew, teechew".
Size of Egg: 14.4—20.1× ×11.3—14.8 mm.

Blue Tit

Paridae

Parus caeruleus

The charming little blue tit is an inhabitant of the whole of Europe, excepting northern Scandinavia. Even in winter it remains in the neighbourhood of its nest and is a frequent visitor to bird tables. It is especially fond of bits of beef fat and peanuts, and its truly acrobatic feats while it feeds are a delight to watch. In early April pairs of birds may already be seen impatiently flying from place to place in gardens, parks and sun--dappled woods, seeking a suitable site for their nest. If there is no nesting box or tree cavity in the vicinity they will be content even with a crack between the boards of a shed, a hollow tree stump or letter box, where they build the nest of moss, well lined with feathers and fine hairs. The ten to sixteen eggs are incubated for twelve to fourteen days by the hen alone. The newborn young are fed countless small caterpillars and insects by both parents. It is quite a task keeping all these hungry mouths filled and thus all the more remarkable that the older birds often raise a second brood in July. The young leave the nest after seventeen to twenty days but continue to be fed by the parents for a short while longer.

Length: 11.5 cm.
Voice: Varied call-notes like "tsee-tsee-tsee--tsit".
Song: A high "tsee-tsee", followed by a long trill.
Size of Egg: 14.0—17.8× ×10.1—13.2 mm.

Swallow

Hirundo rustica

Hirundinidae

Throughout Europe the graceful swallow has left its native cliffside habitat and moved to the vicinity of buildings where it has found more favourable conditions. It generally arrives in early April but the vanguard may appear at the end of March, often to be caught by an unexpected snowfall. The swallow's favourite nesting sites are stables, sties, as well as passages in houses, where it builds its open nest of mud cemented with saliva and strengthened with plant stalks and straw. The female lines it with feathers before laying the eggs, five as a rule, which she incubates alone for fourteen to sixteen days, being fed meanwhile by the male. The young, which first leave the nest after nineteen to twenty-three days, are fed by the parents on insects caught adroitly on the wing. On fledging, the swallows form large flocks that fly to neighbouring ponds in the evening, where they roost in the thick reeds. One fine day in September or October, however, the whole flock suddenly takes off on its long journey to the tropical parts of Africa or even as far away as South Africa. In Transvaal, for instance, a million swallows were once counted roosting in a single place at one time.

Length: 18 cm.
Voice: Oft-repeated "tswit, tswit".
Song: Delicate long and short twittering and warbling notes.
Size of Egg: 16.7—23.0 ×12.2—15.0 mm.

House Martin

Delichon urbica

Hirundinidae

The house martin inhabits all of Europe, Asia as far east as Japan, as well as North-west Africa, where it is to be found near homes. Unlike the swallow it builds its nest on the outside walls of houses and sheds and under balconies, cornices and eaves, frequently in large colonies, the nests being placed tightly one against the other. The nest is made of soft mud which the house martin collects beside puddles, ponds and rivers, picking it up in its beak, mixing it with saliva and pasting little balls of the sticky mass in rows one above the other to form a covered nest with a small entrance hole at the top. The lining is of straw and feathers, often large ones such as those of a hen. The five eggs are incubated for twelve to fourteen days by both birds, who then feed the nestlings flies aphides, mayflies and small spiders floating through the air on their webs. The nestlings take to wing for the first time at the age of twenty to twenty-three days, but they return to the nest to roost for the night for several more days. In September or October the house martin departs for its winter quarters in Africa, south of the Sahara, returning to its nesting grounds at the end of April or early May.

Length: 13 cm.
Voice: A clear "tchirrip" or "tchichirrip".
Song: Twittering.
Size of Egg: 16.1—21.6 ×11.5—14.7 mm. Colour pure white.

House Sparrow

Passer domesticus

Ploceidae

The house sparrow is one of the commonest birds in Europe and Asia, but is also one of the most widespread in all other parts of the world, where it has been introduced by man. It is found in built-up areas and can often be seen performing its courtship antics as early as February — the male hopping about in front of the female with drooping wings and a gallant air. In March the sparrow already starts building its nest of plant stalks, straw, bits of paper and feathers. Finding a site is no problem, the round, untidy structure with side entrance being placed in the branches of a tree, behind a drainpipe or beam, in a tree cavity or wall crevice and even in a nest box. The birds often nest in colonies. The female lays three to eight eggs on the thick feather lining of the nest and both partners take turns incubating for thirteen to fourteen days. The young fledge within seventeen days and leave the nest. Shortly afterwards the parents prepare to raise another brood, sometimes as many as four a year. The diet consists chiefly of seeds, also buds and the green parts of plants, supplemented in summer by insects. The sparrow is mostly a resident throughout the year, although in autumn flocks may form and roam locally around the countryside.

Length: 14.5 cm. Sexual dimorphism. Many individuals are buff coloured.
Voice: A loud "cheep", "chissis", and various twittering and chirping notes.
Size of Egg: 19.1—25.4× ×13.0—16.9 mm. Coloration of the eggs varies greatly. Male in foreground, female behind.

♀

♂

Pied or White Wagtail
Motacilla alba

This species is distributed throughout the continent and may occur near to human habitations particularly in northern Europe, but mostly in the country alongside brooks and ponds. It may be seen in places where livestock is kept, beside stables and in pastures but also in abandoned quarries and ploughed fields. North and eastern Europe is vacated during the winter when the birds move south, but in western Europe it is sedentary. In the autumn and winter it forms large flocks that roost in the rushes and even in trees lining busy streets and greenhouses. During the nesting season it is highly territorial and individual pairs vigorously chase out any intruder that happens to enter their territory. However, should a sparrow-hawk make its appearance all individuals in the neighbourhood may often join forces to mob this dangerous intruder and force him to leave. The white wagtail builds its nest in semi-cavities in walls, on a rafter in a shed, in a stack of wood, etc. The five to six eggs are incubated for twelve to fourteen days by the hen alone, but both parents share the duties of feeding the young for thirteen to fifteen days, bringing them insects and their larvae, which they gather near shallow water.

Length: 18 cm. The female has more grey than the male.
Voice: A lively "tchizzik", alarm an abrupt "tchik".
Song: Is made up of similar notes.
Size of Egg: 16.7—22.3× ×13.1—16.2 mm. Picture shows a white wagtail, distinguished in breeding season from the pied wagtail by its grey rather than black back.

♂

Grey Wagtail

Motacilla cinerea

Motacillidae

This handsome bird with a strikingly long tail which it continually pumps up and down is to be found running about on the boulder-strewn banks of brooks and streams. Here, in the shallow water, it seeks small water-beetles and insect larvae. It also frequents farmyards, searching manure heaps for insects, mainly flies, which it captures skilfully on the wing. However, it always seeks sites near water, building its nest on a beam beneath a bridge spanning a brook, in a hole in the wall left by a dislodged brick, in piles of stones, a semi--cavity in a rock face or in a nest box. Both partners take turns incubating five to six eggs for twelve to fourteen days and both share the duties of feeding the young for twelve to thirteen days in the nest and a few more after they have fledged, following which the parents often have a second brood. The grey wagtail is distributed throughout Europe, except for Scandinavia, and is mostly a resident.

Length: 18 cm. Sexual dimorphism. *Voice:* Call-notes more metallic than in the case of the pied wagtail; alarm a shrill "see-eet". *Song:* Chirping with flute-like notes. *Size of Egg:* 16.1—21.7× ×12.7—16.0 mm. Male in foreground, female behind.

Starling

Sturnus vulgaris

Early in spring we may hear a strange and varied sequence of notes, including sounds resembling the cackling of a hen and pleasant, high flute-like trills, emanating from the top of a tree or from beside a nest-box. All are made by the starling, an excellent imitator of other birds' songs. It has almost entirely abandoned the deciduous woods that were its original habitat and has moved into towns and suburbs. There, from April to June, the female builds the nest of rootlets and dried grass, mostly in wooden nest boxes. She is sometimes assisted by the male. Both share the duties of incubating the four to six eggs, alternating at regular intervals, for a period of two weeks, and both feed the hungry nestlings who welcome each meal of insects and their larvae, molluscs and worms with a harsh, rasping call. The older nestlings literally fight to be among the first to get to the entrance hole with their wide-open beaks. Not till the age of three weeks do they find courage to venture from the nest for the first time. After they have fledged starlings assemble in flocks that visit cherry orchards and in autumn they are frequent and unwelcome visitors to vineyards. The flocks roost in spinneys, reeds or on town buildings and move south and west to escape the cold weather. Some winter in southern Europe and North Africa. Scandinavian populations winter in the British Isles.

Length: 21.5 cm. The female's plumage has a less metallic sheen than the male's.
Voice: A harsh, descending "tcheer".
Song: Whistling and squeaky notes as well as imitations of the songs of other birds.
Size of Egg: 26.2—34.1 × 19.7—23.2 mm.

Swift

Apus apus

Swifts arrive in the skies over their nest sites in May. One may hear their shrill, piercing calls that signal their return from tropical and Southern Africa. These scimitar-winged birds can, if pressed, hurtle through the air at a remarkable speed — up to 160 km per hour. Swifts also possess great endurance and may be able to fly more than 800 km in a single day — a truly unbelievable feat. In the evening one may see them frolicking on the wing and at night they fly to great heights and even sleep in flight. On the ground, however, they are totally inept because their legs are small and weak. The swift builds its nest on tall buildings, in wall crevices and holes beneath eaves, and in old castle ruins. It is constructed of material the bird catches on the wing, such as floating feathers, bits of straw, etc., cemented together with its sticky and rapidly congealing saliva. The clutch consists of two to three eggs, which the female incubates alone for eighteen to twenty-one days, being fed meanwhile by the male who brings her insects caught in flight. The young generally leave the nest at the age of thirty-five to forty-two days and are immediately capable of flight.

Length: 16.5 cm.
Typical features
are the long wings
shaped like
a scythe.
Voice: A shrill,
piercing
"screech
uttered in flight.
Size of Egg:
22.8—28.0
× 14.3—17.6 mm.
Colour white.

Barn Owl

Strigidae

Tyto alba

The barn owl has taken a liking to built-up areas, preferring them to its original cliff habitats. It is fond of barn lofts, attics, dovecots and will even build its nest in church steeples or dark corners of a castle ruin, where its hoarse voice has frightened many a passer-by. It remains faithful to its chosen home, even in winter, but in times of severe frosts and lack of food it frequently migrates. The barn owl is one of the few cosmopolitan species because it is found in all other continents. It is not particularly discriminating as to the time of nesting and its clutch of four to six eggs may be found any time from March to November. When there is an abundance of mice it will have as many as three broods a year. It also hunts rats, bats, sparrows, amphibians and insects. The eggs, often laid in a bare scrape, are incubated for thirty to thirty-two days by the hen, fed meanwhile by the male. The young, which usually fledge after fifty-two to fifty-eight days (this period sometimes being extended to eighty-six days), are fed by both parents. Shortly afterwards the young owls scatter about the countryside.

Length: 34 cm. The facial disk of feathers, generally heart-shaped, is characteristic. Rocking flight. *Voice:* A long, wild shriek, also hissing, snapping and yapping notes. *Size of Egg:* 34.8—43.0× ×28.6—33.5 mm. Colour white.

Kestrel

Falco tinnunculus

Falconidae

High above the field, as if pinned to one spot in the sky, hovers a small predator — the kestrel, its keen eye seeking the ground below for prey. The instant some careless fieldmouse emerges from its underground passage the kestrel quickly swoops down to catch it in its claws. Besides fieldmice it also hunts other rodents, as well as grasshoppers and other insects. It is easy to understand why the bird is the farmer's friend. In late April or early May it builds its nest on a rocky ledge, an abandoned crow's nest, a tree cavity or larger nest box. The female lays five to seven eggs which she incubates for twenty-eight to thirty days. The young, covered with a thick layer of down, are fed by the male for the first few days and later by both parents. At about the age of one month the young kestrels leave the nest, remaining in the company of the older birds until autumn. Birds from northern and north-eastern Europe migrate to southern Europe and North Africa for the winter. Populations inhabiting the other parts of Europe are either resident or roam far afield. Kestrels are also to be found in Asia and Africa.

Length: male 32 cm, female 35 cm. The male has the top of the head coloured blue-grey, the young resemble the female.
Voice: A clear "kee-kee-kee" and a more musical double note "kee-lee"
Size of Egg: 31.9—47.2 ×22.1—36.3 mm.

Spotted Flycatcher

Muscicapa striata

Muscicapidae

From a high perch, such as a cottage roof, wooden fence-post or jutting branch, the spotted flycatcher darts out to catch a butterfly or a fly on the wing, immediately returning to its favourite post. This agile bird may be seen throughout Europe in sparsely wooded regions as well as in parks and gardens. It arrives from its winter quarters in tropical and South Africa at the end of April or beginning of May, building its nest of rootlets, plant stalks and moss lined with vegetable fibres, fine hairs and feathers, in a wooden nest box. Should there be a lack of suitable sites it will even build its nest on a rafter in a shed, over a doorway, or on a horizontal branch jutting out over a much frequented path. The four to six eggs are incubated for twelve to fourteen days, generally by the hen. The parents provide the young with insects, one at a time; considering that a family may consume more than five hundred insects a day, the adults are kept busy. The spotted flycatcher leaves for its winter quarters at the end of August.

Length: 14 cm.
Voice: A rapid "tzee-tuc-tuc" and a grating "tzee".
Song: Soft, thin, high notes that are rarely audible, like "sip-sip-see-sitli-see-see".
Size of Egg: 16.4—21.4× ×12.5—15.6 mm.

♂

Collared Flycatcher

Ficedula albicollis

Muscicapidae

This species is a summer visitor to parts of southern Sweden, Poland, central Europe, south to Italy, the Balkans and the Crimea. It returns from its winter quarters and may be found chiefly in deciduous woodlands but sometimes in large parks, gardens and orchards. Shortly after its arrival it begins looking for a suitable tree cavity or nest box in which to build its nest of moss lined with feathers. If none is available the male, whose responsibility it is to find a site, must be content even with a hole in a tree stump. The hen's task is to incubate the five to eight eggs which hatch after thirteen days. The young are fed insects by the parents, which they catch skilfully in mid-air, and also caterpillars, small spiders and other invertebrates. The parent birds subsist on the same diet. After fourteen to sixteen days the young leave the nesting cavity, continuing to be fed by the parents for several days more. When fledged, the whole family roams the countryside in the vicinity of the nest. At the end of August or in early September the collared flycatcher migrates southwards from its breeding grounds to warmer places.

Length: 13 cm. Sexual dimorphism; the female predominantly brownish.
Voice: A ringing "tschist-tschist" also "whit-whit".
Song: A short "tsit-tsit-tsit-siu-si".
Size of Egg: 14.3—19.7 ×11.5—14.7 mm. Male on trunk, female looking out of cavity.

Garden Warbler

Sylviidae

Sylvia borin

The garden warbler inhabits parks with thick undergrowth, thickets alongside rivers, streams and ponds, as well as hardwood and mixed forests with dense undergrowth. It occurs in almost all of Europe, its distribution extending eastwards as far as western Siberia. It arrives from its winter quarters in Africa anywhere from late April until the middle of May. The fairly large nest may be situated in thickets close to the ground, sometimes in raspberry or blackberry bushes. Both partners share the task of collecting the long, dry plant stalks which form nesting material, interlacing the inner layer with spider and caterpillar webs. Both likewise share the task of incubating the four to five eggs for twelve to fourteen days and rearing the young, feeding them insects, insect larvae and spiders. They are just as conscientious in caring for a young cuckoo hatched from one of the eggs deposited by this parasitic species in their nest. At around eleven to fourteen days (perhaps earlier) the young hop out of the nest though still incapable of flight. Besides insects the garden warbler also feeds on various berries in the autumn. At the end of August or beginning of September it leaves for its winter quarters.

Length: 14 cm.
Voice: Call-note "check-check" also "tchur-r-r" and a faint "whit".
Song: Lengthy, pleasant, loud, flute-like.
Size of Egg: 17.0—23.2× ×13.0—16.5 mm.

Blackcap

Sylviidae

Sylvia atricapilla

The blackcap is common throughout Europe, in Asia as far as western Siberia, in the Middle East and on the coast of Northwest Africa. European blackcaps winter in southern Europe, many also in Africa down the equator, returning in April to their breeding grounds in hardwood and pine forests, groves, parks and overgrown gardens, both in lowland and mountain regions. The blackcap builds a carelessly woven nest of stalks in the forked branch of a bush close above the ground, lining it with horsehair or other animal hairs. The male furthermore builds a special nest for himself where he will perch and sing. Both parents take turns incubating the four to six eggs for a period of thirteen to fourteen days and both feed the young with hairless caterpillars for eleven to fourteen days in the nest, and for a few extra days after they have fledged. In July the blackcap often has a second brood. Adult birds feed chiefly on insects, insect larvae and spiders. They also like blueberries, raspberries and other forest berries; in the autumn they are particularly partial to elderberries. In August or early September, however, they again migrate southwards.

Length: 14 cm. Distinguished by the crown or cap which is brown in the female and glossy black in the male. *Voice:* An emphatic "tac-tac". *Song:* Flute-like notes ending in a loud whistle. *Size of Egg:* 17.0—22.2× ×13.0—15.8 mm. Male in foreground, brown-capped female behind.

Whitethroat

Sylvia communis

Places with thick growths of brambles and nettles are the favourite habitats of the whitethroat, found throughout Europe. In the east its distribution extends to Lake Baikal and it is also widespread in North-west Africa. Its arrival at the end of April or in early May is made known by the cock, who often flies upward in an oblique line, warbling as he goes, and then hurtles down again, continuing his song after landing in the thickets. At other times the cock sings while perched on a high branch, thistle or other tall plant. It builds its nest close above the ground in thickets and hedges (it is particularly fond of brambles, blackthorns and nettles), in groves of trees and on rocky slopes. Sometimes the nest is placed directly on the ground. It is a loosely woven construction of grasses and rootlets, the edges sometimes lined with spider webs. The whitethroat has its first brood in May and a second one in June. The female lays four to six eggs, which both partners take turns incubating, usually for a period of thirteen days. The nestlings are fed with the type of food eaten by the adults — insects and their larvae, small spiders, etc. The young abandon the nest at the age of eleven to thirteen days and in September the birds depart for their winter quarters in Africa.

Length: 14 cm. The female has brownish sides, the male's are tinged pink.
Voice: A quiet but fast "wheet--wheet-whit--whit-whit", also a repeated "check".
Song: Short, repeated melody composed of whistling and flute-like notes.
Size of Egg: 16.0—20.9× ×12.0—15.2 mm.

Lesser Whitethroat

Sylvia curruca

This species is found throughout Europe, excepting Spain and Ireland, from mid-April onwards. In the east its range of distribution extends all the way to northern China. The females arrive about a week after the males, who find the suitable nesting site. The lesser whitethroat is frequently found in parks, cemeteries, overgrown margins of woods and hedgerows. It will only breed in large rambling gardens and its nest is a lovely woven construction built of long and thin rootlets which this small bird plucks out of the ground. Both partners share the duties of incubating the four to six eggs for ten to twelve days. They have one brood in May or June and frequently a second one in July or August. At the age of ten to fifteen days the young leave the nest, continuing to be fed by the parents on small insects, caterpillars and spiders a short while longer. In the autumn the lesser whitethroat also feeds on various berries. In September it departs for its winter quarters in the tropical parts of Africa.

Length: 13.5 cm. The male has a richer coloration.
Voice: Call-notes like "tcharr" or "check".
Song: Begins with subdued warble, followed by outburst of unmusical rattling.
Size of Egg: 14.0—18.9× ×11.5—14.5 mm.

Icterine Warbler

Hippolais icterina

Sylviidae

This species is widespread in central, northern and western Europe, apart from the British Isles. In the east its distribution extends as far as western Siberia. Not until mid-May does it appear in its breeding territory, generally selecting a damp site near a stream or pond. The loud, varied and pleasant song of the icterine warbler may be heard from among the bushes of park and garden or in deciduous woods at almost any time of day. The male changes his perch every now and then, moving from a low bush to the branch of a tall tree and back again. Both partners build the deep, tidy, semi-spherical nest of grasses strengthened with bast and spider webs. The outer walls are often camouflaged with bits of bark, generally birch bark. It is usually situated two to four metres above the ground, often lower, and frequently on the branches of an elderberry bush. The three to six eggs (pink, spotted with black) are incubated by both partners, the male, as a rule, taking over only at mid-day. The young hatch after twelve to thirteen days and leave the nest about two weeks later. Food consists of aphides, flies and other insects. The end of August is the time of this bird's departure via Italy and the Balkans for its winter home in Africa.

Length: 13 cm.
Voice: A musical "deederoid" or "hooeet".
Song: Very loud and composed of phrases in which one can distinguish the songs of other birds.
Size of Egg: 17.0—21.5× ×12.4—14.7 mm.

Chiffchaff

Sylviidae

Phylloscopus collybita

Often as early as mid-March one may hear the monotonously repeated song of the chiffchaff emanating from the tree-tops in parks, gardens and woodlands. It breeds throughout most of Europe after spending the winter months in the Mediterranean. Its distribution also includes North-west Africa and Asia as far as northern Siberia. Though basically a tree dweller it builds its nest on the ground in grass, on gentle slopes, in ditches, beside forest trails, in clearings, etc. It is an enclosed circular construction made of dry leaves and grasses and is so excellently camouflaged that it is very difficult to spot. The entrance, built by the female alone, is a small opening at the side. The six to seven eggs are incubated for thirteen to fourteen days generally by the hen alone and the task of rearing the young is also mainly her responsibility, though the male sometimes assists. On reaching the age of thirteen to fifteen days the young hop out of the nest, although the parents still continue to feed them insects, larvae, spiders, etc. a short while longer. Departure for winter quarters is usually in late September, though some individuals do not leave until November.

Length: 11 cm.
Weight: A mere 8 to 9 grams.
Voice: A soft "hweet".
Song: Monotonous, continually repeated "chiff-chaff-chiff-chaff".
Size of Egg: 13.0—17.7× ×10.5—13.7 mm.

Nightingale

Turdidae

Luscinia megarhynchos

Bushes on the edges of damp, deciduous woods, overgrown parks, gardens, hillsides and thickets bordering rivers and ponds are favourite haunts of the nightingale, whose clear pure song fills the night and may also be heard at intervals during the day. But not all nightingales have the same sweet song, and some are markedly more accomplished than others. Nightingales return to their breeding grounds, embracing all of Europe except Scandinavia, Ireland and Scotland, from mid--April onwards, flying, as a rule, by night. First to arrive are the males, which immediately burst into song. The females arrive several days later. The nest is built of grass, rootlets and dry leaves close to the ground or on a pile of leaves, well concealed in thick undergrowth. The female lays three to six eggs which she incubates herself for fourteen days. However, in rearing the young, which hop out of the nest at the tender age of eleven days, though as yet incapable of flight, she is aided by the male. Both parents feed the young with insects, larvae, spiders, etc. In late August or early September the nightingale leaves for its winter home, migrating to tropical Africa.

Length: 16.5 cm.
Voice: A liquid "wheet", short "tuc", etc.
Song: Beautiful, rich and varied melodies alternating with joyous bubbling phrases; the song often includes melodies learned from other birds.
Size of Egg: 18.2—24.7× ×13.9—17.0 mm.

Dunnock

Prunellidae

Prunella modularis

In parks, gardens, cemeteries, as well as deciduous and coniferous woods, one may chance upon the large nest of the dunnock located in dense undergrowth or in the branches of a spruce. In woodlands the basic building material consists of dry spruce branches, in gardens long bean stalks, elsewhere the stems of nettles; failing these the nest is made mostly of green moss. The lining is likewise of fine moss with which the dunnock's four to five blue-green eggs blend so well as to be practically invisible. The task of incubating the eggs falls mainly to the hen, though the male relieves her at regular intervals during the twelve- to fourteen-day period. When they are twelve to fourteen days old the young birds leave the nest, being fully able to fend for themselves soon afterwards. Although the population is large, a dunnock concealed in a thicket may easily escape notice. The staple diet consists of insects, larvae and spiders, and in autumn berries and seeds as well. In September or October it leaves the more northern regions for the western and southern parts of the Continent, occasionally wintering as well in central Europe and returning to its breeding grounds in March or April.

Length: 14.5 cm. Overall coloration greyish.
Voice: A high, piping "tseep" and trilling note.
Song: Sharp, loud, metallic notes.
Size of Egg: 17.5—21.2× ×13.0—15.5 mm.

Marsh Tit

Parus palustris

Paridae

Most of Europe, except the northernmost regions, is home for the agile marsh tit, an all-year-round resident. Favourite haunts are parks and large gardens, but it also inhabits deciduous and mixed woods. The individual pairs remain together even during the winter months, often joining other tits and forming groups that roam the countryside. In early spring, usually the beginning of April, the marsh tit claims its nesting ground and at the end of the month or the beginning of May the hen lays six to twelve eggs. The nest, made of moss and thickly lined with hairs, is generally located in a cavity, the tit being satisfied even with a hollow in a tree stump or rotting branch and, if nothing else is available, a nest box. The eggs are incubated for fourteen days by the hen alone, the young leaving the nest at the age of eighteen to nineteen days, but continuing to be fed insects and larvae by the parents for a short while longer. The adult birds also feed on various invertebrates, and in autumn and winter add small seeds to their diet. In winter the marsh tit is a frequent visitor to parks.

Length: 11.5 cm.
Voice: A loud "pitchew" or "piti-chewee", sometimes also "chick-adeedee-dee". It is, however, only rarely heard.
Song: Melodic warbling.
Size of Egg: 14.6—17.1 × × 11.5—13.1 mm.

♂

Long-tailed Tit

Aegithalos caudatus

Aegithalidae

The long-tailed tit is one of the smallest of European birds, weighing a mere eight to nine grams. Unlike other tits, it does not make use of simple cavities but builds an elaborate nest. This is a closed, egg-shaped structure about twenty centimetres high, with a small entrance at the top, made of moss, lichen and spider-webs. The outside is camouflaged with bits of bark and the inside is lined with masses of assorted small feathers, sometimes numbering more than a thousand. Both partners share the task of building the nest, the male bringing the material and the female shaping it, the work taking from fifteen to twenty days. When it is completed the hen lays six to twelve small eggs which she incubates alone for a period of twelve to thirteen days. The young are fed small insects by both parents while they are in the nest and for a while after fledging. As a rule, the adult birds then have a second brood, though the young of the first brood remain in their company. The latter have even been seen assisting their parents in feeding the new nestlings. On fledging the long-tailed tits form small groups that roam the countryside, flitting from tree to tree. They remain in their breeding territory even in winter.

Length: 14 cm. Distinguished by small round body and unusually long tail.
Voice: A repeated "tsirrup" and a weak "tsee--tsee-tsee". It may be heard even in flight.
Size of Egg: 12.8—16.0× ×10.0—12.0 mm.

Waxwing
Bombycilla garrulus

This bird inhabits the coldest northernmost parts of Europe and Asia. It also occurs in North America, where it is known as the Bohemian waxwing. Waxwings live in coniferous and mixed woods where they build nests of twigs and moss in the branches of trees, usually in the Arctic summer, i.e. June or July. The clutch comprises four to five eggs incubated by the female for a period of fourteen days, during which time she is fed by the male. Both parents feed the young nestlings with insects and larvae. At the age of sixteen to eighteen days the young leave the nest and form flocks, sometimes numbering as many as several thousand birds. In October, as a rule, they set out for central Europe where they remain until March. In some years they may move as far west as the British Isles in some numbers. At this time they may be seen in tree-lined avenues, and in parks and gardens, especially on shrubs such as viburnum and cotoneaster (feeding on the berries). An observer may approach close to a flock of waxwings without their taking wing for they are fearless and inquisitive by nature. The waxwing has an enormous appetite, food passing through the alimentary canal very rapidly. Indeed it spends most of the day hunting for food, only occasionally taking time to rest on a branch.

Length: 18 cm.
A gregarious bird usually congregating in flocks. The male's plumage is brighter than the female's. A distinctive feature is the long red-brown crest.
Voice: Call-note a weak trill "zhree".
Size of Egg:
20.7—28.3×
×15.6—18.8 mm.

♂

Short-toed Tree Creeper

Certhia brachydactyla

Certhiidae

The short-toed tree creeper hops in spirals up a trunk like a small mouse. On reaching the top it flies down to the foot of another tree and resumes its climb, sharp claws catching in the bark while stiff tail feathers provide the necessary support. Food is largely comprised of insects, as well as their eggs, larvae and pupae, pecked out of the cracks and crevices in the bark with the long, narrow, down-curved bill. In summer it also feeds on aphides, bed bugs, small beetles and caterpillars and is regarded as one of the most beneficial birds of parks and gardens. It is also found, however, in thin deciduous woodland as well as pine forests. In April the female builds the nest under a loose piece of bark, in a crack in a tree trunk, in a stack of wood or even a wall crevice. Placed on a foundation consisting of a high pile of dry twigs, it is constructed of grass, moss and lichen, the hollow lined with soft, fine materials, mostly hairs. It is amazing how such a small bird can cope with such a task. The six to seven eggs are incubated for thirteen to fifteen days, usually by the hen alone, though both parents share the duties of feeding the young on small insects and larvae.

Length: 12.5 cm. General colour brownish.
Voice: Call-note a high "srrieh".
Song: A rhythmic "teet-teet--teeteroititt".
Size of Egg: 15.4—17.4× ×11.0—12.6 mm.

Greenfinch

Carduelis chloris

*Fringillidae*

The greenfinch is a fairly common bird occurring in parks, large gardens, avenues, orchards, as well as margins of forests and sun-dappled groves of trees. It usually stays the winter, though northern populations migrate south and west. Sometimes finches form flocks that roam far afield throughout the countryside, returning to their nesting grounds in early April. The nest of twigs and roots, with a soft lining of feathers, hairs and horsehair, may be found in thick hawthorn bushes by the roadside, in conifers or even in fruit trees. The five to six eggs are incubated by the hen, which is fed by the male during the thirteen- to fourteen-day period. Both parents share the duties of rearing the young, feeding them mostly with crushed seeds and an occasional caterpillar or spider. Adult birds also feed principally on the seeds of various plants, shrubs and trees. The young leave the nest at the age of fourteen days, though yet incapable of flight, perching on nearby branches for a few more days and waiting for the titbits brought them by their parents. In July or August the greenfinch generally has a second brood. In the winter months it is a frequent visitor to feeding trays.

Length: 14.5 cm. The general coloration of the female is greyish. *Voice:* A repeated short "chup" or "ten", also a rapid trill. *Song:* Various bell-like notes. *Size of Egg:* 17.2—24.1 × ×12.2—16.1 mm.

98

European Goldfinch

Fringillidae

Carduelis carduelis

The European goldfinch is a very attractively coloured songbird. Its range includes all of Europe except the northernmost parts. It is rarely to be seen during the breeding season, however, even though it may nest in parks and gardens. An extremely wary bird, it remains well concealed and sometimes only its song betrays its presence. The nest, built by the hen, is likewise well masked, and needs an expert to find it. The outside of the nest is woven of lichen and leaves; if located in a pine tree, pine needles are also used. In gardens the European goldfinch is fond of placing its nest on the branch of a plum, apple or cherry tree; in parks on a maple or poplar. The duties of incubating the five to six eggs are performed by the hen alone for twelve to fourteen days, fed on the nest by the male. The newly-hatched young are fed aphides and, later, partially digested seeds by both parents. After they have fledged they form small flocks that roam the countryside even during the winter months. They often visit thistles and burdock, expertly extracting the seeds, and are also fond of the seeds of alder, birch, etc.

Length: 12 cm. The female is paler than the male.
Voice: Frequently repeated liquid twittering "swilt-witt-witt--witt".
Song: Composed of foregoing notes.
Size of Egg: 15.6—20.0× ×12.3—14.3 mm.

Linnet

Fringillidae

Acanthis cannabina

Open country, small woods, fields, hedgerows and hillsides covered with thickets, as well as overgrown parks, gardens and cemeteries are frequented by the linnet. It is distributed throughout all of Europe except northern Scandinavia. It also occurs as far as western Siberia and southward to the Canary Islands. In the temperate regions it is either resident or migrates locally; in more northern territories, however, it migrates south for the winter. In the autumn linnets form groups that often join up with other seed-eating finches and buntings. In April the birds make for their nesting grounds and immediately begin building their nests of plant stalks and roots lined with plant wool, horsehair, etc., normally placing them among the thick branches of evergreen trees, in shrubs, one to two metres from the ground, and sometimes, though rarely, in blackberry bushes. Built by the hen alone, but with the male in constant attendance, the nest is completed within two days. Both partners share the duties of incubating the five to six eggs for a period of eleven to fourteen days and also of feeding the young. The diet consists of various seeds, partially digested in the crop of the older birds. Adults feed mostly on the seeds of plants such as dandelion, plantain and thistles, sometimes on green shoots and occasionally on insects.

Length: 13 cm. The female has a paler crimson breast patch and cap or lacks them altogether.
Voice: Usual call "tsooeet" or a rapid twitter.
Song: Loud, flute-like notes including some learned from other birds.
Size of Egg: 14.7—22.2× ×11.2—14.9 mm.
Male in foreground, female behind.

Serin

Serinus serinus

Fringillidae

Not yet established properly as a breeding species in the British Isles and Scandinavia, the serin inhabits most of Europe. The end of March marks its return from southerly regions to its breeding grounds. In towns, especially in parks and gardens, its pleasant twittering song may be heard daily. When singing, the male is fond of perching on a slender branch or telegraph wire. As soon as the trees and bushes are covered with leaves the hen begins building the small nest on a horizontal branch. It is made of thin rootlets, plant stems, bast and leaves, and lined so expertly with feathers and plant wool that the three to five small eggs are practically invisible. The task of incubation for a period of eleven to thirteen days likewise falls to the hen alone, the male, however, meanwhile feeding her regularly. The young leave the nest at the age of eleven to fourteen days, by that time having trampled it so that it looks like a flat platform. On fledging serins gather in flocks that roam the countryside, feeding on the seeds of thistles, alders and birches, after first removing the husks. In October they migrate to their winter quarters in southern Europe.

Length: 11.5 cm. The female is paler than the male and the head is covered with dark spots.
Voice: A rapid "si-twi-twi-twi" or a hard "chit--chit-chit".
Song: Chirping twittering.
Size of Egg: 14.4—17.6× ×11.0—12.7 mm.

Chaffinch

Fringilla coelebs

One of our commonest birds, the chaffinch, is found not only throughout Europe but also in North-west Africa, the Middle East and Asia as far as western Siberia. Birds inhabiting northern areas migrate to the Mediterranean in the autumn. In the remaining regions they are resident or migrate only locally. The males stake out their nesting grounds in February or March. The females arrive somewhat later, selecting a nesting site, usually in the fork of a branch, and then building the nest, mostly alone, the male assisting only for brief intervals. It is a neat compact cup of moss, lichen, spider webs, etc., often camouflaged with bits of bark from the tree in which it is placed. The chaffinch has one brood in April or May and a second one in June or July. The clutch usually comprises five eggs, incubated for twelve to fourteen days by the hen alone. Both partners, however, share the duties of rearing the young, feeding them mainly on insects and spiders for about two weeks in the nest, and for a short while after they abandon it. The diet of adult birds consists mainly of seeds. On fledging chaffinches form groups that roam the fields with other seed-eating birds or frequent parks and gardens where there are feeding trays or bird tables. They are also plentiful in thin woodlands.

Length: 15 cm. The male's plumage is brighter, the female's duller and greyer.
Voice: The well known "chwink--chwink".
Song: Short, melodious and rattling, terminates in a well defined flourish.
Size of Egg 17.0—22.8 ×13.2—15.8 mm. Male in front, female behind.

Tree Sparrow

Passer montanus

Ploceidae

The tree sparrow is widespread throughout Europe and Asia, its range extending as far as Japan. Birds inhabiting southern regions and areas with a milder climate are resident; only northern and eastern populations are migratory. In winter groups of these sparrows roam the countryside, often in the company of siskins, seeking various seeds, mainly those of weeds. During this period they roost in piles of twigs, thick treetops and cavities of various kinds. At the beginning of spring, often as early as February, the female perches on the branch of a tree, fluttering her wings, uttering soft cries and thus enticing the male to her side. During the breeding season the tree sparrow builds its nest in tree hollows in orchards, parks, forest margins, etc. It may also select a hole in the wall or even the lower part of a stork's or eagle's nest. Frequently it is a colonial nester. Both partners share the duties of building the nest which is made of bits of straw, hairs, feathers, etc. The clutch comprises five to six eggs, incubated in turns for thirteen to fourteen days by both parents. In spring and summer the birds feed on insects and larvae, later on plant seeds.

Length: 14 cm.
Voice: A short "chick" or "chop", in flight "tek tek".
Song: Comprised of similar notes.
Size of Egg: 12.5—22.3× ×10.4—15.5 mm. The coloration of the eggs varies considerably.

Rook

Corvus frugilegus

As winter draws in the skies are filled with clouds of rooks migrating from northern and eastern Europe. Populations inhabiting the central and western parts of the Continent migrate only locally. At this time, especially towards evening, huge flocks may be seen winging their way south. During the day they visit fields and meadows and at night they roost together in the woodland treetops. In early spring these huge communities break up into smaller flocks that fly to their regular breeding grounds where they nest in colonies. The nest, built in the tops of old trees, is made of twigs broken from the tree with the strong bill. Sometimes, however, the birds repair the previous year's nest instead of building a new one. Often as early as the end of March the hen lays four to five eggs which she incubates alone for eighteen days. The male brings her food during this period and sometimes she flies off the nest to meet him. When the young hatch the male feeds the whole family for several days on his own, but about six days later the hen also shares the task. Almost ninety per cent of the food consists of harmful insects, especially cockchafers, carried by the adult birds in a special throat sac. The diet is supplemented by various seeds.

Length: 46 cm. Adult birds have a bare, white skin at the base of the bill (the cere).
Voice: Usual notes "kaw" or "kaaa".
Size of Egg: 32.2—47.4× ×25.2—30.4 mm.

Jackdaw

Corvus monedula

Corvidae

The jackdaw may site its nest in old castle ruins, a large park with plenty of old, hollow trees, a tree-lined avenue, an abandoned quarry, on a cliff edge or even on a church steeple. A gregarious bird, it breeds in loose colonies, occasionally in very large ones. In April or May individual pairs start building their nests of twigs, broken from the tree, in various hollows and crevices. The lining consists of a layer of straw, hairs and feathers. The clutch usually comprises five or six eggs and the parents share the duties of incubating for seventeen to nineteen days, though the male sits on the eggs only for brief periods. The diet consists of insects, especially beetles, worms and molluscs, as well as frogs and other small vertebrates. The adults also feed on seeds and are fond of visiting cherry orchards as well as gardens where there are ripe strawberries. When seeking their food they fly close to the ground. At the age of one month the young leave the nest and a few days later may already be seen flying about the neighbourhood. Soon afterwards the jackdaws form larger groups, often joining flocks of rooks. The jackdaw is distributed throughout Europe except northern Scandinavia. Northern populations winter in central and western Europe.

Length: 33 cm. The male and female have similar plumage. Young birds lack the grey on the sides of the neck. *Voice:* A clear, repeated "chak" also "kya". It also learns to imitate other calls and even human words. *Size of Egg:* 30.0—40.9 ×21.6—29.7 mm.

Collared Dove

Streptopelia decaocto

Columbidae

Today the collared dove inhabits the whole of Europe including urban neighbourhoods. It may be found in parks, gardens and avenues, even in large cities, as well as on a single tree in a town square. It is a resident bird, remaining for the winter and forming large flocks wherever there is ample food, as around farmyards, poultry farms, zoos, etc. In cities the collared dove will even perch on windowsills and accept titbits, from seeds to scraps from the dinner table. Seeds, in fact, form the principal item of diet, supplemented by insects, molluscs and worms. The nest is built in the branches of tall bushes, sometimes on a windowsill, on the sheltered top of a nest box or feeding tray, etc. It is a simple, haphazard construction made only of dry twigs placed on top of one another. The hen generally lays two eggs, which she and her mate take turns incubating for a period of fourteen to fifteen days, the young nestlings fledging three weeks later. The collared dove has as many as four broods a year and the nest may be found even in winter. The main breeding season, however, is from April to September.

Length: 28 cm. In winter it forms flocks.
Voice: Typical a deep "coo-coo-coo", in flight a nasal "kwurr".
Size of Egg: 27.5—33.8 ×21.8—25.0 mm. Pure white.

Grey-headed Woodpecker

Picidae

Picus canus

The grey-headed woodpecker is widespread in eastern and central Europe, its distribution extending as far as eastern France and south-western Scandinavia. In the British Isles its place is taken by the green woodpecker, a species with more red on the head and heavier black moustachial stripe. In large parks, in deciduous and mixed woods and even high in the mountains one may hear the drumming noise made by this bird in early spring as it chips at the rotting trunks of oaks, alders, birches, willows and fruit trees to chisel a cavity (sometimes as much as 50 cm deep) for its nest. Both partners perform this task, though the male does the major share of the work. The job is completed after about two weeks, the male often making another cavity for himself in which to sleep. The five to ten eggs, lying on a small pile of splinters, are incubated for seventeen to eighteen days by both partners who also share the duties of feeding the young on a diet consisting mainly of ants and ant cocoons. At the age of twenty-five days the nestlings leave the nesting cavity, returning there, however, for the night. In winter the grey-headed woodpecker usually lives a solitary life. Both it and the green woodpecker are fond of attacking ants' nests, often on lawns. However, both like to feed also on seeds. In autumn they pay frequent visits to orchards.

Length: 30 cm. The female lacks the red on the head.
Voice: In spring four to ten notes "doo doo doo doo . . ."; also "laughing" notes.
Size of Egg: 24.3—30.0× ×19.0—21.6 mm. Male on trunk, female looking out of the nest.

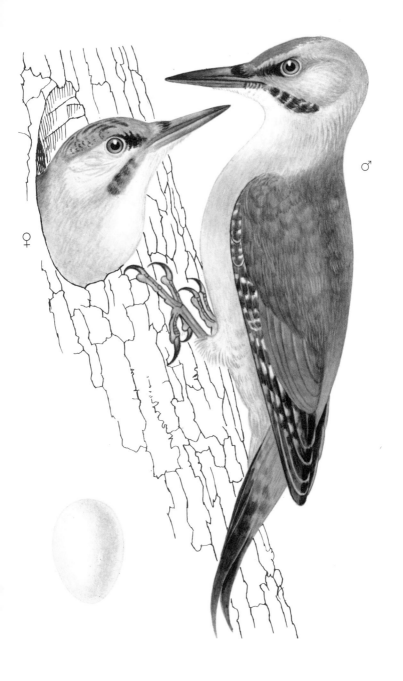

Lesser Spotted Woodpecker

Dendrocopos minor

Picidae

The lesser spotted woodpecker is to be found throughout Europe, in Asia as far as Japan and in North-west Africa, though it is nowhere abundant. It frequents broad-leaved and mixed woods in lowland areas, though it also visits old parks, tree-lined avenues, and orchards. It is a resident bird, but those that breed in northern areas migrate to central Europe. In winter it roams the countryside, often in the company of tits. During the courting season from March to April it often drums softly on dry stumps of branches. Both partners chisel a ten- to fourteen- centimetre- deep nesting cavity in rotting tree trunks or branches anywhere from near ground level up to twenty metres high. This task is undertaken afresh every year. Both share in incubating the four to seven eggs for a period of two weeks and feeding the young, the diet consisting of insects (mostly gall-flies) larvae, cocoons and to a lesser degree, ants. The nestlings leave their shelter for the first time at the age of three weeks. In winter the lesser spotted woodpecker feeds principally on the eggs and cocoons of insects,which it finds in crevices in the bark of trees, and also seeds.

Length: 14.5 cm. The adult female lacks the red on the crown.
Voice: A repeated high "pee-pee--pee". It may be heard drumming from early spring until autumn.
Size of Egg: 17.0—21.0× ×12.9—15.6 mm. Male perching on trunk, female in nest.

Wryneck

Jynx torquilla

Picidae

In the second half of April one may hear the monotonous, querulous call of the wryneck in gardens, orchards, parks and avenues of trees, as well as in deciduous and mixed woods. Because the bird varies the intensity of its call now and then one is led to believe that it is close at hand one moment and far off the next, but the wryneck is probably perched motionless on a branch at the top of a tree, on a telephone pole or on some other vantage point. Surprisingly, the female may be as vocal as the male. Both birds prepare a nest of a few shavings or small bits of rotting wood in a cavity selected by the hen. This may be in a tree hollow, an opening in loose masonry or a sparrow's nest box (the occupants of which are if necessary often unceremoniously dislodged). Male and female take turns sitting on the eggs, seven to ten in number, for twelve to fourteen days; and both share the duties of feeding the young, their diet being the same as that of adult birds — mostly ants and their cocoons. The wryneck gathers these by breaking up an anthill and collecting the inhabitants on its long sticky tongue. It also feeds on other insects, however, and in autumn on the fruit of the elderberry. When disturbed on the nest it stretches its neck out and hisses like a snake, thus often frightening the enemy. The wryneck leaves its breeding grounds in Europe in August or September to winter in North Africa or farther south in the tropical regions.

Length: 16.5 cm. Though a member of the woodpecker family, it does not chisel its own cavity.
Voice: A repeated "kyee-kyee".
Size of Egg: 16.2—23.0× ×13.0—16.7 mm.

Little Owl

Athene noctua

Strigidae

Sometimes, walking in a park or on the edge of a forest, one may be struck by the great flurry and agitated cries of a group of small birds which without any apparent reason suddenly converge on a particular spot in the bushes or in a tree. A moment later the cause of the furore is revealed as an owl flies up and away, looking for a sheltered spot where it can hide from its pursuers. The raptor involved is the little owl, found throughout Europe, except in Ireland and Scandinavia, on open, rocky country, in abandoned quarries, margins of forests and overgrown parks. It builds its nest chiefly in a tree hollow and will take over wooden nest boxes. From four to eight eggs are laid on the bare ground without any lining and incubated by the hen for twenty-six to twenty-eight days. On hatching, the young are covered with a thick coat of down and are fed with insects and small vertebrates by both parents. They leave the nest at the age of twenty-eight to thirty-five days, already capable of flight. The little owl hunts insects, mainly cockchafers, at dusk and fieldmice and rodents at night, so that it is genuinely a useful bird. Sometimes, especially when rearing and feeding the young, it even hunts during the day. It is a resident, although sometimes it migrates locally and occasionally flies up to two hundred kilometres or more from its nesting ground.

Length: 23 cm.
Voice: A shrill "kiu", a sharp "werro", etc.
Size of Egg: 31.5—37.1 ×25.7—31.0 mm.
Colour white.

♂

Barred Warbler

Sylviidae

Sylvia nisoria

The barred warbler is abundant in central and eastern Europe, but absent from the British Isles, much of France and Spain as a breeding species. Its distinguishing feature is the bright yellow eye and barring which resembles that of the sparrowhawk. It migrates in late August and in the course of the journey often visits western Europe — British Isles, France, Holland, etc. — before continuing to its winter quarters in East Africa and southern Arabia. It returns to its breeding grounds again in early May. The barred warbler inhabits open country with bush cover, being particularly fond of fields bordered by small woods and hedgerows. It often builds its nest close to that of the red-backed shrike, chasing the latter away with vigour should it come too close. The nest, woven of dry grasses and lined with hairs or plant fibres, is generally placed close to the ground in dense thickets. The usual clutch consists of five eggs, incubated by both partners for a period of two weeks. The young are fed with insects and other invertebrates and at the age of fourteen to sixteen days leave the nest, remaining a short while longer in the company of their parents. During the breeding season the male sings from a high branch and may be seen as he flies up at a tangent and back again to his perch.

Length: 15 cm. The female has less distinct barring on the underside, the young lack it altogether.
Voice: A hard "tchack", also "tcharr-tcharr".
Song: Melodic, often including the "tcharr" notes.
Size of Egg: 18.0—23.1× ×14.0—16.4 mm.

Marsh Warbler

Acrocephalus palustris

Sylviidae

Moist, overgrown ditches and fields are the marsh warbler's favourite habitats. It is widespread in western Europe (though restricted to the southern counties of England), central and eastern Europe, as far as western Siberia. In Scandinavia it occurs rarely and only on the south coast. In the middle of May it returns to its breeding grounds from its wintering zone in East Africa, having journeyed there the previous year at the end of August or beginning of September. Shortly after its arrival it starts building a typical nest of grass and other plant stalks in tall grass, cereal crops bordering rivers, as well as clover. The nest is built very close to the ground, not above water, and either among tall, standing plant stems, or among dwarf shrubs and dense growths of tall nettles. In May or June the hen lays four to seven eggs which she and the male take turns in incubating for a period of twelve to thirteen days. The nestlings, which leave their shelter at the age of eleven to thirteen days, are fed with small insects and larvae, these also being the staple diet of adult birds. After hatching, the young are fed by the parents for some ten days more. The marsh warbler's song may be heard even at night.

Length: 12.5 cm.
Voice: A loud "tchuc", "tweek", etc.
Song: Resembles that of the mocking-bird but lacks the chirping notes of other birds.
Size of Egg: 16.7—21.5× ×10.0—14.9 mm.

Whinchat

Saxicola rubetra

At the end of April or in early May the whinchat, which spends the winter in North Africa, returns to its breeding grounds in fields, meadows and moors. It favours hilly country with isolated trees and bushes. In spring one may see it perching on a telephone wire, the top of a shrub or any piece of high ground where it has a good view. The instant it spots a fly or other insect, it swoops to the attack. The nest is built in a shallow depression in the ground, well concealed in a thick clump of grass or under a low bush. The four to seven eggs, usually unicoloured blue-green, are incubated by the hen alone for a period of twelve to fourteen days. The young hop out of the nest when they are about twelve days old, as yet incapable of flight, and conceal themselves in various nearby places. Even when they have fledged, however, they continue to be fed by the parents who teach them how to catch insects on the wing. At the end of August or beginning of September the whinchat journeys south again for the winter. It is widespread through nearly all of Europe, and in Asia ranges as far as the western parts of Siberia; it is also found in south-western Asia.

Length: 12.5 cm. The female's plumage is more sober than the male's.
Voice: A short "tic-tic" or "tu-tic-tic".
Song: Whistling and grating notes somewhat reminiscent of the black redstart.
Size of Egg: 15.2—21.5 ×12.9—15.4 mm.

Stonechat

Saxicola torquata

Dry open meadows with low shrubs, stony and barren sites, as well as heathland, are the favoured habitats of the stonechat. It is widespread in western, central and southern Europe and also in many places in Asia and Africa. Birds inhabiting central Europe migrate to the Mediterranean for the winter whereas western and southern populations are resident. At the end of March the stonechat may already be seen back in its breeding grounds, the male perching on a large stone or horizontal branch of a bush, singing his spring song. In April or May it sets about building its nest of rootlets and stalks, lined with animal hairs and other soft materials and excellently concealed in a clump of grass, the overhanging stems forming a kind of roof. The three to seven eggs hatch after fourteen to fifteen days, being incubated by the hen alone. The young leave the nest at the age of twelve to thirteen days, as yet incapable of flight, concealing themselves amongst the stones in the surrounding grass. In June or July many pairs have a second brood. The diet consists of small insects, larvae, spiders, worms and small molluscs. In winter the stonechat frequents fields and meadows.

Length: 12.5 cm. The female is not as brightly coloured as the male and lacks the black head. *Voice:* "Wheet--tsack-tsack". *Song:* A short repeated, grating "wheet-wheet". *Size of Egg:* 15.6—20.0× ×13.2—15.5 mm. Male on stem, female on nest.

Wheatear

Turdidae

Oenanthe oenanthe

The wheatear is found on open steppeland, in mountain areas, among rocks and dunes, in abandoned sandpits and quarries, and on railway embankments. Its range includes all of Europe and Asia, North Africa and even Greenland. European birds migrate in late August or the beginning of September to North Africa, returning at the end of March or beginning of April. The wheatear is essentially a ground bird, running about with agility or perching on a large stone which affords a good view of the surroundings. In May or June it builds its nest in a pile of stones, a rock crevice, a hole in the ground or even between railway sleepers. Made of roots, plant stalks and small twigs, and lined with animal hairs and feathers, it generally contains five to seven eggs which hatch after thirteen to fourteen days. They are incubated mostly by the hen, the male taking part only occasionally and for a short time. However, both partners share the duties of rearing the young, bringing them beetles, butterflies, caterpillars and other invertebrates. The diet of the adult birds is the same. The young hop out of the nest when they are two weeks old but do not begin to fly until a few days later.

Length: 14 cm. The female is not as brightly coloured as the male.
Voice: A hard "chack" or "weet-chack".
Song: Simple, grating, seemingly suppressed notes, heard only rarely.
Size of Egg: 18.4—23.2× ×14.0—16.5 mm.

Great Grey Shrike

Lanius excubitor

Laniidae

The great grey shrike is the only shrike that stays for the winter in its breeding ground, which includes most of Europe except for the British Isles and Italy. It is also found in Asia, North Africa and North America. In winter it roams the neighbourhood, frequenting shrubbery, fields and meadows and feeding chiefly on fieldmice, often hunting its prey by hovering motionless in the air. When food is plentiful it has the habit of impaling it on sharp thorns, often establishing quite a large cache on a single bush. In summer, however, it also hunts and impales lizards, various insects and sometimes even young birds. The nest of dry branches and roots, lined with feathers and hairs, is built in April or May, usually in a tree two to five metres above the ground. The hen lays three to six eggs which she incubates mostly herself, the male relieving her only occasionally. Should a crow or magpie appear in the vicinity of the nest during this period of fifteen to sixteen days, both partners fly quickly to the attack and chase the intruder away. The young remain in the nest until they are nineteen or twenty days old, continuing to be fed by the parents, however, for another three weeks.

Length: 25 cm.
Voice:
Characteristic
"shek-shek".
Song: Croaking
and whistling
notes as
well as those
learned from
other birds.
Size of Egg:
23.0—30.5
×18.0—20.7 mm.

Woodchat Shrike

Lanius senator

Laniidae

The woodchat shrike likes warmth and does not return until the beginning of May to its nesting grounds, which are confined to southern and south-west Europe and the warmer areas of central Europe. It also occurs in North-west Africa and the Middle East. Dry open country with isolated trees and shrubs, fields with concealing undergrowth, the fringes of woods and, above all, south-facing slopes regularly warmed by the sun, are the bird's favourite haunts. Shortly after its arrival it starts building the nest in bushes and trees (including fruit trees and, in the south, olive trees). It is made of roots and dry plant stalks and lined with hairs, feathers and horsehair. The edges are often "decorated" with green leaflets. The clutch, numbering five to seven eggs, is incubated by the hen alone for a period of fourteen to sixteen days. The young leave the nest when they are about twenty days old. The parents continue to feed them for another three weeks whilst teaching them to catch prey such as insects and spiders. Adult birds will even attack a small lizard or fieldmouse, and sometimes the chicks of smaller birds. At the end of August or beginning of September the woodchat shrike departs for its winter quarters in tropical Africa.

Length: 19 cm.
Voice: Warning — a yapping "shek-shek".
Song: Varied, with notes learned from other birds.
Size of Egg: 21.0—27.0× ×15.7—17.8 mm.

136

Red-backed Shrike

Lanius collurio

In hedgerows and forest margins one may some-times come across beetles, grasshoppers and other insects impaled on the spikes of thorny shrubs — a grisly kind of entomological collection. It is, in fact, a cache prepared by the red-backed shrike for leaner days. The nest, built in similar surround-ings and well concealed in the undergrowth, is made of roots, dry stalks and other plant material and lined with a soft layer of hairs and plant wool. The major share of the work is undertaken by the male and is completed within three to four days. The three to eight eggs are incubated chiefly by the hen for a period of fourteen to fifteen days. The male only relieves her on rare occasions. Both partners, however, share the duties of feeding the young, chiefly with insects and larvae. At the age of two weeks the young already perch neatly beside one another on branches outside the nest, but they continue to be fed by the parents for three weeks more until they are fully independent. On approaching the nest one may hear the bird's typical call of warning but the male's song is hard to distinguish for it is an excellent mimic of other birds' songs. In August the red-backed shrike leaves for its winter quarters in tropical and south-ern Africa, returning fairly late, in mid-May.

Length: 18 cm.
Sexual dimorphism.
Voice: A harsh, grating "shack-shack" or "chee-uk".
Song: A soft chatter with melodies learned from other birds.
Size of Egg: 18.3—26.1 × × 14.0—19.0 mm.
Male in foreground, female behind.

♀

♂

Brambling

Fringilla montifringilla

Fringillidae

Every year the brambling makes the long journey from its breeding grounds in Scandinavia to northern Asia for the winter. The huge flocks, sometimes numbering several thousand individuals, are often heading south by the end of September. At this time they may be seen in central and southern Europe where, together with other finches, they visit stubble and ploughed fields and meadows. They also feed on the berries of the mountain ash, or on the seeds of alders and birches. When snow covers the ground, solitary bramblings will visit feeding trays, even in large cities and villages. As soon as winter is over (March — April) the brambling returns to its home in the far north where it nests in coniferous forests. The nest of moss and plant stalks is camouflaged with lichen from the tree in which it is placed. In June the female lays four to seven eggs, incubating them alone for fourteen days. The nestlings are fed with insects and larvae by both parents, leaving the nest at the age of thirteen to fourteen days but continuing to be fed for a short time after fledging. Soon after this they congregate in large flocks.

Length: 15 cm. The female does not have the glossy blue-black crown.
Voice: A metallic "tsweep", also "tchuc".
Song: Chattering and bell-like notes.
Size of Egg: 18.1—22.2× ×13.5—15.6 mm. Male above, female below.

♂

♀

Skylark

Alauda arvensis

Alaudidae

High in the sky, almost motionless, hovers the skylark, its sweet liquid song filling the air. Between May and July it has two, sometimes three broods. The nest of roots and bits of leaves, lined with hairs and horsehair, is placed on the ground in fields and meadows. The male carefully guards his territory, fiercely fighting to defend it against his rivals. The hen lays three to five eggs which she incubates alone for a period of twelve to fourteen days. The young are fed with various insects and larvae, centipedes, spiders and small snails by both parents. They leave the nest at the age of nine to eleven days, though as yet incapable of flight, and conceal themselves in clumps of grass. When three weeks old, they are not only able to fly but also to feed themselves. Adult birds also eat the seeds of various weeds which they gather on the ground. In October — November skylarks form small groups which fly off together to their winter quarters in southern Europe, returning sometimes as early as the end of February when the tang of winter is still in the air and snowfalls not uncommon. Its range of distribution includes the whole of Europe, a large part of Asia and North-west Africa.

Length: 18 cm.
Voice: A clear, liquid "chir-r-up".
Song: Trilling and warbling; sometimes notes learned from other birds.
Size of Egg: 19.4—28.0 ×15.0—19.5 mm.

Crested Lark

Alaudidae

Galerida cristata

On the mainland of Europe one may sometimes come across a pair of crested larks running to and fro along a road, even in a busy city street. In winter the bird is often found in built-up areas, seeking for seeds on the ground. With the arrival of spring, sometimes even in early March, the birds (which pair for life) get ready to nest near rubbish dumps and highways, on railway embankments and in other localities resembling their original habitats on the eastern steppes, the region from which they spread to Europe in the fourteenth century. They were, for example, first sighted in Cologne on the Rhine in 1552. In Denmark they arrived much later, around 1850; and they have yet to make their appearance in the British Isles. The nest, a careless construction of stalks and roots, is built on the ground by the female, with the male in attendance. The four to five eggs hatch after twelve to thirteen days, incubation being undertaken principally by the hen, relieved by the male only occasionally. She likewise rears the young, which leave the nest when nine days old, as yet incapable of flight, fledging at the age of eighteen days. The crested lark is mainly a vegetarian, though the young are fed only on insects and worms.

Length: 17 cm. Distinguishing feature is the conspicuous crest.
Voice: A liquid "twee-tee-too".
Song: Slightly resembling that of the skylark with notes learned from other songbirds.
Size of Egg: 19.0—24.8× ×15.0—18.3 mm.

♂

Tawny Pipit

Anthus campestris

Motacillidae

The tawny pipit inhabits dry, open country — stony slopes, abandoned sandpits, steppes, sandy heaths, etc. Nowadays its range includes the whole of Europe except Scandinavia and the British Isles, even though it did at one time nest in England (in Sussex, in 1905—6). The bird can also be found in North-west Africa and in Asia. It returns to its breeding grounds at the end of April or in early May and builds its nest on the ground in a depression beneath a clump of heather, dwarf shrub or behind a larger mound or stone. It is made of moss and roots, lined with a soft layer of hairs and is well concealed by overhanging grass. Only the female does any building work and it is she who incubates the four to six eggs for a period of thirteen to fourteen days, relieved on rare occasions by the male. The diet consists mainly of insects and larvae, particular partialities being beetles and locusts, hunted on the ground. The young leave the nest at the age of fourteen days but remain in the neighbourhood. In August or September they migrate to North Africa or Arabia, where they feed mainly on various kinds of grasshoppers.

Length: 16.5 cm.
Voice: Rare variable call-notes such as "tsweep", "chup", "chirrup", etc.
Song: A repeated metallic "chivee-chivee-chivee".
Size of Egg: 19.0—23.8× ×14.2—17.1 mm.

Yellowhammer

Emberiza citrinella

Emberizidae

From April to July, throughout Europe, one can hear the typically monotonous yet pleasant, wheezing song of the yellowhammer perched in the top of a thicket, in a hedgerow, the edge of a wood or similar places. During this period it has two broods. When courting, the male hops about, circling the hen with drooping wings and ruffling his bright chestnut rump. He often enhances his attractions by picking up a stem and prancing about with it in his beak. The nest of stems, stalks and roots is built in the grass or close to the ground, as, for example, on the branch of a spruce. It is almost always lined with horsehair, though it is a mystery how the birds find this material. The clutch comprises three to five eggs incubated mostly by the hen, though the male assists now and then. The young hatch after twelve to fourteen days and leave the nest twelve to fourteen days after that, continuing to be fed by the parents for another ten days. About thirty per cent of the diet consists of insects, worms and spiders; the rest is comprised of seeds. After fledging, the birds gather in small groups to visit fields and meadows. In winter they often frequent the outskirts of cities.

Length: 16.5 cm. The female is more soberly coloured than the male.
Voice: A metallic "chip".
Song: Monotonous "chi-chi-chi--chi-chi-chweee" (a little bit of bread and no cheese!). While singing the male perches on a high branch.
Size of Egg: 18.0—25.9× ×14.3—17.8 mm.

Ortolan Bunting

Emberiza hortulana

In the seventeenth century the ortolan bunting, originally a native of grass and brushlands, began to spread to Europe from the east. In the nineteenth century it appeared in Germany and has since penetrated to western Europe, though not thus far to the British Isles. It inhabits dry, open country with isolated thickets, fields, meadows and tree--lined avenues, and is often found in vineyards. It is a migratory species and returns to its breeding grounds at the end of April or in early May. Shortly after its arrival it sets about building its nest on the ground, in a hedgerow, on arable land or on fallow ground concealed by grass and other plants. It is interesting to note that the male is not particularly aggressive in defending his territory and two or three may often be found singing on the same tree without any sign of enmity. The four to six eggs are incubated by the hen. The young hatch after twelve to thirteen days and are fed on small locusts, grasshoppers and other insects. The diet of the adult birds, though it includes these items, consists chiefly of various plant seeds. When the nestlings have fledged, families of ortolans congregate in flocks that journey in August or September to their winter quarters in Africa (south of the Sahara) and Arabia.

Length: 16 cm. The female is more soberly coloured than the male and has a spotted throat.
Voice: A soft "tsee-ip".
Song: Slow and variable, final note lower or higher.
Size of Egg: 18.0—22.5× × 14.3—17.0 mm.

Cirl Bunting

Emberiza cirlus

Emberizidae

This bunting, distinguished by its handsome colouring, inhabits western and southern Europe and the southern half of the British Isles. It stays for the winter in its breeding grounds, gathering in flocks that visit fields and meadows. It frequents open country with isolated shrubs and trees, cultivated areas, vineyards, woods and tree-lined thoroughfares. The female builds the nest of stalks in a concealed spot on or just above the ground (a clump of grass or a thicket) and lines it with fine stems, horsehair, etc. She incubates the three to five eggs for eleven to thirteen days, raising one brood in April and often a second one in June. The young leave the nest at the age of ten to fifteen days. They are fed chiefly on insects and larvae. In addition to these items the adults feed on various small seeds and berries in the autumn and winter. In places where the species is common, it is the male that usually attracts notice, for he is fond of singing on a high perch.

Length: 16 cm. The rump is olive-grey, the female lacks the black spot on the throat.
Voice: A weak "sip-sip".
Song: Twittering syllables "cirrrl".
Size of Egg: 19.2—24.0× ×15.0—18.0 mm.

Snow Bunting

Plectrophenax nivalis

Emberizidae

The snow bunting inhabits the far northern parts of Europe, Arctic Asia and North America, sometimes nesting high in the mountains of northern Scotland. Every year in September or October it migrates south in huge flocks. At this time it may also be seen inland but it does not stay long, wintering mainly in areas bordering the coasts of the North Sea, the Atlantic, the Baltic and the Mediterranean. In April it returns to its breeding grounds, frequenting the rocky valleys of rivers and streams as well as mountains up to the snowline. The female usually builds the nest well secreted between stones, in rock crevices or among shrubs growing on rock faces. It is made of moss, lichen and grass and lined with hairs, horsehair, feathers and plant wool. Four to six eggs are laid during the brief Arctic summer (June or July) and incubated by the hen for about fifteen days. The young leave the nest after the same length of time. The staple diet consists of insects, larvae and other invertebrates, but adults also feed on small seeds. The snow bunting is fond of hunting mosquitoes near water, catching them on the wing.

Length: 16.5 cm. The female is brown, the breeding male black and white. *Voice:* A loud "tsweet" and "ten". *Song:* A high, rapid "turi-turi--turi-tetitui". *Size of Egg:* 19.5—25.1× ×14.3—18.0 mm. Picture shows male in non--breeding (spring) plumage.

Magpie
Pica pica

The magpie is notorious for its habit of collecting glittering objects which it then conceals in various hiding places. Whereas wild birds are very shy and wary, individuals reared in captivity are quickly tamed and grow into entertaining companions, though one must be careful to keep objects such as eyeglasses, rings and spoons out of sight. The magpie is widespread not only in Europe but also in Asia, North-west Africa and North America. It stays for the winter, roaming the countryside far and wide in small flocks of ten to twenty individuals. In Europe its favourite haunts are shrub--covered hillsides, woods and the edges of ponds. In early April individual pairs build their nest in a tree or tall shrub. It is made of dry, mostly thorny twigs, lined with turf and loam with an inner layer of hairs and fine stalks. It is additionally protected by a kind of roof made of thorny twigs. The hen lays three to ten eggs which she incubates for seventeen to eighteen days, mostly on her own. The young are fed in the nest by both parents for twenty-four days and for a short period after fledging. The diet consists of mice, fieldmice, lizards, insects and other invertebrates, as well as seeds, fruits and berries.

Length: 46 cm. Distinguishing feature is the long tail. Young birds are coloured black but lack the glossy sheen.
Voice: Raucous, barking cries "chak-chak--chak".
Size of Egg: 27.3—41.9× ×21.2—26.4 mm.

♂

Stone Curlew

Burhinus oedicnemus

Burhinidae

Open fields, but especially sandy and dry localities, are the favourite haunts of the stone curlew, a sturdy bird with large, yellow, owl-like eyes, inhabiting southern, eastern and western Europe (including south-east England) and sometimes central Europe. It is quite common in places but because of its predominantly nocturnal habits may easily escape notice. In more southerly areas it is a resident species. The northern populations migrate to Africa in September or October, returning to their breeding grounds in April. Some individuals also winter in south-west Europe. The nest, without any lining, is built in a shallow depression on the ground. The hen lays two and sometimes three spotted eggs, usually in May. Some pairs have a second brood in July. Both partners share the duties of incubating for a period of twenty-five to twenty-seven days. Towards evening the stone curlew ventures out to hunt beetles, locusts, worms and other invertebrates, and occasionally small lizards and rodents. It is a very active bird capable of running rapidly on the ground and also an accomplished flier. Its call is heard mainly at dawn and dusk.

Length: 40.5 cm. Conspicuous in flight are the two white bands on the wings.
Voice: A wailing "coo-ree" or a high shrill "keerrr-eee".
Size of Egg: 47.0—61.7 ×35.6—43.0 mm.

158

Corncrake

Crex crex

Rallidae

Late in the evening, walking along a path in a field, one may suddenly hear strange sounds resembling the scraping of a comb against the edge of a matchbox. It is in fact the call of the corncrake, returned from tropical Africa to its breeding grounds in Europe. It arrives about the middle of May and, unlike its relatives, seeks out dry sites in fields and meadows. It is mostly heard on warm nights after dark as well as early in the morning before dawn. The simple nest, lined with bits of leaves and grass stems, is placed in a well concealed depression in field or meadow. The clutch usually comprises six (but sometimes as many as eighteen) eggs which are icubated by both partners for a period of nineteen to twenty--one days. The nestlings are entirely black and leave the nest the day after hatching, running about close by. For the first few days they are fed on caterpillars, beetle larvae, small spiders, etc. by the parents. Later they themselves hunt various insects and worms on the ground and sometimes gather seeds as well. They are capable of moving rapidly through thick stalks of standing grain because the sides of their bodies are flattened.

Length: 26.5 cm.
Voice: "Rerrp rerrp rerrp . . .", carrying a great distance, especially at night.
Size of Egg: 31.4—41.6× ×24.1—29.0 mm.

Great Bustard

Otididae

Otis tarda

The steppes of western Asia, Asia Minor and North-west Africa, as well as certain parts of the flat farmlands of central Europe, are the habitats of the great bustard. In former times this huge bird of the grasslands was far more widespread in Europe and in the eighteenth century it was found even in the British Isles. It generally stays for the winter in its breeding grounds, congregating in small flocks that roam the fields and meadows. In spring the male performs his typical courtship display on the ground, inflating his throat pouch and spreading his wing and tail feathers to form a fan so that from a distance he looks like a large black-and-white "dancing" ball. The males wage fierce battle amongst themselves to win the favour of the hen. Hers is the task, in April or May, of preparing a simple hollow in the corn or tall grass in which she generally lays two eggs, incubating them for twenty-five to twenty--eight days. The spotted nestlings are very independent. Their diet comprises chiefly insects and later plant food. Adult birds occasionally catch small vertebrates. Nowadays the great bustard is protected in most of Europe. Attempts have also been made to reintroduce the species to the British Isles.

Length: Male — 102 cm, female — 80 cm. The male weighs up to 15 kg whereas the hen weighs only 4 to 6 kg. *Voice:* Low, bellowing sounds. *Size of Egg:* 69.0—89.5× ×51.5—63.1 mm.

Partridge
Perdix perdix

Phasianidae

In many parts of Europe the common partridge is a favourite and important game bird. In some central European countries it is even captured live and exported. A resident species throughout Europe, it is to be seen during winter in small groups, usually families. Because it frequents snow-blanketed fields and meadows during the winter months it relies to a considerable extent on food put out for it in sheltered spots. Early in spring the groups break up. Young birds begin their search for a mate, adults remaining paired for life. In May or June the hen prepares the nest, lined with grass and leaves, in a deep hollow, concealed in a clump of grass or under a shrub. She incubates the eight to twenty-four eggs for twenty-three to twenty-five days while her mate stands guard close by. The nestlings, which feed themselves, are reared by both parents; if the hen dies then the male continues alone. The diet consists of insects and green leaves at first and is later supplemented by seeds. The young birds fledge at the age of sixteen days. Adult birds feed on seeds, insects, worms, spiders and molluscs and nibble green food.

Length: 29 cm. The male has chestnut shoulders whereas the female's have ladder-like markings. The female may also have the "horseshoe" on the breast.
Voice: A grating "krrr-ic" or "kar-wic".
Size of Egg: 31.6—40.4 × 24.1—29.4 mm.

164

Quail

Coturnix coturnix

Phasianidae

Until a short time ago the quail was found in large numbers throughout Europe, the Middle East, and as far east as Japan. In southern Europe and North Africa more than twenty million of these small fowl-like birds were shot and eaten every year. Such large-scale killing naturally took its toll and their numbers rapidly diminished, even though they are still fairly abundant in places. The quail is the only gallinaceous bird of Europe that is a migrant, leaving for its winter quarters in North Africa and Arabia in the autumn and returning at the end of April or beginning of May. Its favourite haunts are steppes, fields and dry meadows. Quails do not pair for life and a male often has several hens. These, however, must incubate the six to eight eggs and rear the young themselves. The tiny nestlings, spotted golden-brown, hatch after seventeen to twenty days, fully capable of feeding themselves from birth. They catch small insects and larvae, snip off bits of green leaves and later also gather seeds. At the age of nineteen days they are already capable of flight and congregate in small groups until they migrate in the autumn. Populations inhabiting southern Europe and Africa are resident.

Length: 17.5 cm. In spring the male has two chestnut-brown or brownish-black stripes on the neck, the hen is more speckled.
Voice: Characteristic trisyllabic call of male "whic-whic-ic". Heard long distances until late summer.
Size of Egg: 25.0—33.9× ×20.0—25.0 mm.

FEEDING BIRDS IN WINTER

Many birds are resident, remaining in their nesting grounds throughout the winter, no matter how cold the weather. Others, whose diet consists of berries, remain as long as there is enough for them to feed on and then fly off to seek food elsewhere. Finally there are the birds such as fieldfares and redwings that inhabit the far north, up to and beyond the Arctic Circle, and migrate south in flocks, remaining in central and southern Europe for the winter.

Among resident species are most tits, as well as nuthatches and woodpeckers. So too are many seed-eaters, such as the greenfinch, chaffinch, siskin, goldfinch, bunting and sparrow, all of which roam the countryside, usually in small flocks, throughout the winter, often visiting gardens. Their numbers are increased by such northern guests as the redpoll, brambling and bullfinch.

As a rule birds have no difficulty obtaining food in winter as long as there is not too much snow and the ground and trees are not coated with ice (as, for example, after a sudden thaw). Tits and tree creepers pick concealed insects or their eggs and cocoons out of cracks in the bark, but a coat of ice often blocks their access to food. Many seed-eaters are likewise deprived of nourishment when there is a deep layer of snow for they generally seek their food on the ground where many grass, alder and birch seeds are to be found.

When bad weather lasts a longer time the birds are hard put to find food and many of them die of hunger. At such a time city outskirts and houses are visited by large numbers of woodland birds and the provision of food saves many from starving to death. Some birds, such as young tits, that have not yet raised a brood and have no nesting ground, will become accustomed to the place where they find food in winter and will settle permanently in the neighbourhood.

Fig. 4. Garden feeding tray

Birds, however, cannot be fed only on bits of bread. For the majority crumbs make a totally unsuitable diet (exceptions being house sparrows, starlings and collared doves). Natural food is by far the best, especially seeds, provided, of course, that they are not mouldy or rancid. Oil seeds in particular provide birds with ample calories in winter. Seeds are eaten in winter also by birds which otherwise, in spring and summer, feed mostly on insects (tits, nuthatches, woodpeckers). Sunflower seeds are ideal for these species. A tit will take one at a time from the bird table and fly off with it to a nearby tree where, supporting itself on its feet, it cracks the hard shell with its bill and eats the sweet, oily kernel. The nuthatch, on the other hand, places the seed in cracks or holes in the bark and then proceeds to crack the shell and eat the seed inside. Hemp seed is also suitable but as this has a hard shell it should be slightly crushed before being served to the birds. Birds may be fed millet, canary seed, flax seed, rape seed, hulled oats and poppy seed. The collared dove also eats wheat and maize. In addition one can provide them with the seeds of grass, thistles and conifers as well as rowan, hawthorn, elderberries and the like, dried during the late summer months. Tits also appreciate bits of beef or mutton fat and an occasional mealworm.

Some birds, like the goldfinch, will only rarely visit bird tables. For these it is possible to cut off whole thistle and teazle branches in the autumn and store them until the winter months. Then, in the winter, they can simply be stuck upright into the snow. Food is usually put out for birds in a feeder made of wood, which should be topped with a small roof to protect the contents from rain and snow. Sometimes feeders are constructed with an entrance at the bottom, the birds flying in from below, and the feeding space proper enclosed with glass (Fig. 4). Such a feeder also provides protection against the wind and birds can take shelter there in harsh weather. Equally suitable are automatic feeders with a larger supply of seeds in a reserve container from which they automatically drop as soon as those in the tray have been consumed. They can be brought from pet shops or through bird protection societies. Such feeders must, of course, be replenished regularly.

PRACTICAL PROTECTION OF BIRDS

Many useful birds, mainly insectivorous species, are diminishing in number every year. They build their nests in dense thickets where they forage for food and keep their stores (as, for example, the shrike and its impaled insects). Their homes in the undergrowth, alongside roads, on the margins of forests, etc., are being destroyed by the intensive cultivation of farmland and they are gradually being deprived of their natural environment. Since many are unable to adapt themselves to the new conditions as successfully as did the sparrow, they are abandoning their homes and moving to other areas. The shrike has an inborn instinct to build its nest in thorny thickets in open country and cannot live, for instance, in a spruce wood, nor will it build its nest on the ground in a field, like the lark; the latter, by the same rule, would not nest in thickets. Individual pairs of nesting birds cannot move to the remaining suitable localities for each pair requires a specific space for nesting and this cannot be decreased to any great extent. The only remaining way to preserve birds in their original homes is to plant trees and thickets on such land as cannot be used for agricultural purposes — on slopes bordering roads, in abandoned quarries, alongside brooks and streams and on field boundaries. Not only will many birds build their nests here but these places will also provide shelter for wild game such as hares and deer.

Best suited for the purpose are shrubs that bear edible fruits or berries, especially in autumn and winter, such as hawthorn, snowberry, blackthorn, privet, cornel cherry, elderberry, sweetbriar and dogwood, and trees such as mountain ash, birch and alder. Field boundaries should also include several small oaks, lime trees, pines and spruces in whose thick branches many birds build their nests. Naturally, the planting of field boundaries is not primarily an individual concern but the responsibility of nature conservationists and local authorities.

Nevertheless, even the individual can contribute to the protection of birds nesting in thickets, mainly by planting green hedges around the edges of gardens and parks. The best hedges are hornbeam, common maple, privet and dogwood, perhaps with climbing ivy in between. It is important, however, to trim the hedges every year, for this makes them thicker. Incidentally, green hedges as well as single trees and shrubs in gardens will attract many birds that feed on harmful insects — an added boon. Particularly suitable for this purpose are ornamental spruce trees with close-set branches as well as thujas and various juniper trees. Warblers are often quite satisfied with thick gooseberry bushes.

Widely varied species of birds seek the sanctuary of parks and large gardens thickly set with ornamental shrubs and shade-giving trees as well as conifers. Even woodland birds sometimes make their homes there for the environment is similar to their native habitat and affords countless opportunities for nesting. Owls, too, may be found there as well as cuckoos and colonies of rooks that often roost in the tall trees. This is one of the principal reasons why such oases of greenery in the heart of large cities should be cherished.

Special note should be taken of birds nesting in cavities. Natural cavities are to be found chiefly in old trees, which householders often cut down, thus depriving the birds of nesting opportunities. Some seek substitutes such as a hole in a hollow tree stump or pile of stones but the clutch is vulnerable to attacks by small predators that have easy access to such nests. Stray cats are also liable to destroy them.

Tits, typical tree cavity nesters, are very plentiful and play an important role in the biology of life in the wild. They are among the best eradicators of harmful insects. A simple act such as putting out a nest box and food during the winter months can help to increase their number to such an extent that they will play a great part in helping to check insect over-population. Nest boxes especially attract the great tit and blue tit to the garden — in fact any box will do, whether made by hollowing out a tree trunk or by nailing together a few boards. The former most resembles a natural cavity for only the roof is made of wood and fashioned so that it can be opened by tilting up or sliding out to make cleaning easier. However, it requires quite a bit of work and it is liable to crack in the second year if the trunk does not happen to be sufficiently dry. On the other hand, nest boxes of wood are very easy to make and can be constructed of inferior wood. The boards should be placed close together without any cracks in between and the bottom should be fitted between the walls to prevent entry of water during a downpour. Two or three small holes should be bored in the bottom, however, to allow any water that might have penetrated to run out. The roof should be either removable or fastened with hinges so that it can be opened.

The entrance hole should be located in the upper third of the box wall, best of all in the centre, though it may just as easily be made in the corner. A natural entrance hole is always circular, but many birds have no objection to a square one. A perch should not be put in front of the hole for it not only hampers the bird's entrance (it flies straight into the hole), but also makes it easier for pests to get in.

Nest boxes should not be nailed directly to a tree branch but onto a baseboard that may be attached front to back or even from the side. Some boxes may also be suspended from the branch.

The best kind of box for a blue tit or other small bird measures 12 centimetres square and 20 cm high with an entrance hole 26 mm in diameter, hung $1\frac{1}{2}$ to 5 metres above the ground. There is no danger of its being usurped by a sparrow for the latter cannot squeeze through such a small opening.

For the great tit the nest box should be the same size, though it may be 5 cm higher, but with an entrance hole 32 to 35 mm across. Other tits, the collared flycatcher, pied flycatcher and sometimes even a tree creeper or redstart may nest there. In gardens even sparrows will use such a comfortable refuge. The great tit, however, is not one to be put off by such an intruder and if it takes a liking to the nest it will chase out the sparrow, throw out its nest and build one of its own out of moss.

Nest boxes 15 cm square and 28 to 35 cm high with an entrance hole 50 mm across are favoured by the starling, but may be used also by the nuthatch and sometimes even the great spotted woodpecker. Woodpeckers, however, often chip the opening with their strong bills and thus sometimes wreck the box. For that reason in neighbourhoods where woodpeckers are plentiful it is worth making a double front wall or nailing a piece of plywood with a hole of the same size on the outside. These boxes should be hung 3 to 8 metres above the ground.

The largest nest boxes are 20 to 30 cm square and 35 to 40 cm high with an entrance hole 90 to 130 mm across. The occupants of such boxes include the jackdaw, kestrel, owl and other larger birds nesting in cavities. The boxes should be hung 6 metres or more above the ground. The entrance hole may be square and located in the upper corner of the front wall.

Slightly different are the so-called semi-nest boxes sought out by birds nesting in semi-cavities, such as the redstart, wagtail and collared flycatcher. Such a box is 12 cm square and 12 cm high and the front wall reaches only midway. It should be hung 1½ to 4 metres above the ground under the eaves of low buildings, on the walls of cottages, woodsheds and the like. For redstarts and wagtails one can also make semi-cavities in walls.

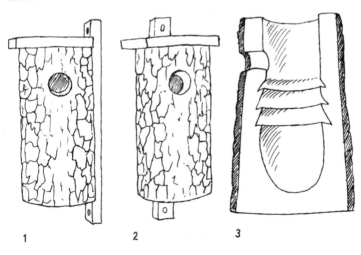

1   2   3

Fig. 5. a, b) Nest boxes, c) section

The swallow and house martin can likewise be helped in finding a suitable place to build their nests of mud. For the swallow, which likes to nest inside buildings, in passageways and stables, one can attach a wooden board to a wall or ledge; for the house martin, which nests only on the outside walls of buildings, some kind of bracket under the eaves or balcony is necessary to serve as a support for the nest, for being made of mud, the latter might dry out and, failing to adhere to a smooth wall, drop to the ground together with the nestlings.

Nest boxes should be hung in places not easily reached by cats and small predators. If put up in a tree, the trunk can be encircled with a protective band of wire mesh or twigs over which such enemies cannot climb.

Furthermore, nest boxes should not be hung close to each other for, as has already been said, birds have their specific nesting territories. Boxes are generally spaced 30 to 40 metres apart (in woods this distance should be greater). The end of

Fig. 6. Semi-nest box

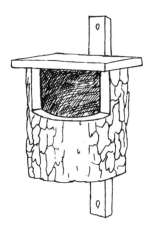

February is the best time to put them up. At the same time old boxes should be repaired and cleaned, for birds will not nest, as a rule, in soiled boxes. Hornets sometimes build their nests there in the summer and the remains of these should also be removed.

BIBLIOGRAPHY

Austin, O. L.: *Birds of the World*. London, 1963.

Bannersman, D. A.: *The Birds of the British Isles*. Edinburgh, 1954.

Benson, S. V.: *The Observer's Book of British Birds*. London, 1937.

Berndt, R. and Meise, W.: *Naturgeschichte der Vögel;* 3 vol. Stuttgart, 1959—1966.

Bruun, B. and Singer A.: *The Hamlyn Guide to Birds of Britain and Europe*. London, 1970.

Creutz, G.: *Geheimnisse des Vogelzuges*. Die Neue Brehm-Bücherei. A. Ziemsen Verlag, Wittenberg, 1954.

Deckert, Gisela: *Der Feldsperling*. Die Neue Brehm-Bücherei. A. Ziemsen Verlag, Wittenberg, 1968.

Dementjev, G. P. and Gladkow, N. A.: *The Birds of the USSR;* 6 vol. Russian. Moscow, 1951—1954.

Gilliard, E. T. and Steinbacher, G.: *Knaurs Tierreich in Farben. Vögel*. Munich and Zurich, 1959.

Glutz von Blotzheim, U. N.: *Die Brutvögel der Schweiz*, Aarau, 1962.

Hanzak, J.: *Das Grosse Bilderlexikon der Vögel*. Bertelsman Lesering. Artia, Prague, 1965.

Heinroth, O. and M.: *Die Vögel Mitteleuropas;* 4. vol., 2nd edition. Edition Leipzig und Harri Deutsch, Frankfurt a. M., 1966—1968.

Heyder, R.: *Die Amsel*. Die Neue Brehm-Bücherei. A. Ziemsen Verlag, Wittenberg, 1953.

Jespersen, P.: *The Breeding Birds of Denmark*. Copenhagen, 1946.

Lincoln, F.: *Migration of Birds*. London, 1950.

Makatsch, W.: *Die Vögel in Feld und Flur*. Neuman Verlag, Radebeul, 1970.

Makatsch, W.: *Die Vögel in Haus, Hof und Garten*. Neuman Verlag, Radebeul, 1970.

Makatsch, W.: *Wir bestimmen die Vögel Europas*. Radebeul, 1966.

Mauersberger, G.: *Urania Tierreich. Vögel*. Leipzig—Jena—Berlin, 1969.

Menzel, H.: *Der Wendelhals*. Die Neue Brehm-Bücherei. A. Ziemsen Verlag, Radebeul, 1968.

Niethammer, G.: *Handbuch der Vögel Mitteleuropas*. Adapted by K. Bauer and U. Glutz von Blotzheim; 2 vol. Frankfurt a. M., 1966.

Nowak, E.: *Die Türkentaube*. Die Neue Brehm-Bücherei. A. Ziemsen Verlag, Radebeul, 1965.

Peterson, R. T., Mountfort, G., Hollom, P. A. D.: *Birds of Britain and Europe*. London, 1971.

Rudebeck, G.: *Studies of Bird Migration*. London, 1950.

Schildmacher, H.: *Wir beobachten Vögel*. Jena, 1966.

Schneider, W.: *Der Star*. Die Neue Brehm-Bücherei. A. Ziemsen Verlag, Radebeul, 1960.

Schütz, E.: *Vom Vogelzug. Grundriss der Vogelzugskunde*. Frankfurt a. M., 1952.

Siefke, A.: *Dorn- und Zaungrasmücke*. Die Neue Brehm-Bücherei. A. Ziemsen Verlag, Radebeul, 1962.

Van Ijzendoorn, A. L.: *The Breeding Birds of the Netherlands*. Leiden, 1950.

Voous, K. K.: *Atlas of European Birds*, London, 1960.

Witherberger, H. F.: *The Handbook of British Birds*. London, 1949.

INDEX OF COMMON NAMES

INDEX OF LATIN NAMES